CHILDREN
STORM

OF
THE

THE AUTOBIOGRAPHY OF NATASHA VINS

journeyforth®

Greenville, South Carolina

Library of Congress Cataloging-in-Publication Data

Vins, Natasha, 1952-
   Children of the storm : the autobiography of Natasha Vins.
     p. cm.
Summary: The autobiography of Natasha Vins, which describes the
persecution of her Christian family while living in the Soviet Union.
   ISBN 1-57924-854-3 (perfect bound pbk. : alk. paper)
   1. Vins, Natasha, 1952- 2. Baptists—Soviet Union—Biography.
[1. Vins, Natasha, 1952- 2. Baptists. 3. Women—Biography] I. Title.
   BX6495.V52 A3 2002
   286'.1'092—dc21

                         2002007681

Visit bjupress.com to access a free discussion guide or to purchase the
BJ BookLink: *Children of the Storm*, an in-depth study of the
autobiography.

Children of the Storm: The Autobiography of Natasha Vins

Translated from Russian by Jane Vins Comden
Designed by Chris Hartzler
Photographs courtesy of Natasha Vins and Unusual Films
Map by Jim Hargis

© 2002 by BJU Press
Greenville, South Carolina 29614
JourneyForth Books is a division of BJU Press

ISBN 978-1-57924-854-3

15   14   13   12   11   10   9   8

To Jane,
wonderful sister,
treasured friend

CONTENTS

PREFACE

November 1975

Our airplane was descending toward the Yakutsk airport. A stewardess announced, "The temperature in Yakutsk is minus fifty degrees." Through the airplane window I could see the snow-covered airfield and a small airport terminal. My whole family—all six of us—had come here to Northern Siberia to visit our father, who was serving a five-year term at the strict-security prison camp. By now we had been traveling for more than twenty-four hours. First we had taken an overnight train from Kiev to Moscow, followed by a ten-hour flight to Yakutsk, crossing five time zones.

The youngest in the family, three-year-old Alex, was fascinated by every little detail of our journey. He had never before been on a train or airplane. When we boarded an overnight train in Kiev, it was impossible to pull him away from the window before it got completely dark. But mostly Alex was excited that he was going to see his Papa. He was only two when Papa was arrested and could hardly remember him.

In Moscow the bus ride from the train station to the airport had taken over an hour. When we boarded the bus, most of the seats were already taken, and Mama, with Alex on her lap, ended up in the very front beside a woman with a five-year-old daughter. Right away Alex started talking to the little girl. Together they looked out the windows and shouted excitedly, "Look, look at that car! And there's a cat! Look there—two boys are coming home from school!"

People on the bus smiled as they listened to the children's cheerful voices. Suddenly Alex asked, "Are you going to visit your Papa in prison?" The little girl looked at him, puzzled. But her mother understood his question very well. She abruptly turned her daughter away from Alex and would not let the children talk to each other anymore. The other passengers also gave Alex and Mama startled looks. But for Alex this was a natural question: since his Papa was in prison, other children's fathers had to be there as well.

Finally our long journey was over, and we arrived at the prison camp. At the entrance the guards checked our passports and led us into the meeting room where our belongings were searched. A few minutes later Papa walked in wearing his black prison uniform. Seeing him, Alex quickly hid behind Mama's back. It took a while for a three-year-old boy to call this stranger "Papa" for the first time.

Unlike Alex, we did not need to get re-acquainted with Papa. We welcomed him with hugs and kisses. Then we all knelt, and Papa thanked God for our family reunion. After the prayer we started to unpack. Papa changed into his regular clothes that we had brought from home. We wanted him at least during our short visit to feel more at home and not be reminded of prison by his uniform.

The barracks for family visits was located inside the prison camp. In it were several rooms and one big communal kitchen. Three other families had arrived before us and were already visiting with their relatives. We were allowed to use two rooms since there were seven of us. The rooms were small. Each had two narrow metal beds with a narrow space between them, a rough wooden table, and two stools. When we had dinner, we moved the table between the two beds, which served as our seats along both sides of the table.

After the first excitement of seeing Papa settled down somewhat, Mama went to the kitchen to make dinner. I helped her, frequently coming back to our room to get more supplies out of our suitcases. Each time I enjoyed seeing a peaceful family scene: Papa was talking to Peter; little Alex was on Papa's lap feeling completely comfortable by now; Lisa and Jane were setting the table. We always brought a tablecloth and a vase that we filled with wildflowers in the summer or pine sprigs in the winter.

When dinner was served, our time around the table was filled with endless conversations. So much had happened while we were separated from Papa! After dinner Mama pulled candies, cookies, and fruit from the suitcase, and we spent hours drinking tea and talking. But for little Alex and Jane it was too boring just to sit and listen as the adults talked. They wanted to move around and play. Jane spoke up first, "Papa! Will you play with us?" Papa cheerfully agreed, and playful roughhousing followed. The little ones squealed with delight when they were able to "wrestle" Papa down.

During such happy moments I struggled with the thought that in just two days our visit would be over. The guards would take Papa back to his barracks, and we would trudge through the snowed-in town to catch a bus to the airport. And once again we would be separated from Papa for many months. . . .

I had to stop myself: it was better not to allow such thoughts to spoil the bright moments of this day.

At bedtime Papa said to Jane and Alex, "Now I will tell you a story about a cat who appeared one night inside our prison camp! And another story about a little palm tree." Jane and Alex jumped eagerly onto the bed where Papa was sitting and clung to him. Papa was ready to begin his story when Peter asked with twinkling eyes, "Is this story only for the little ones? Or may we also listen?"

"Peter," Papa smiled, "we've discussed so many things already! Yes, this story is first of all for Alex and Jane."

He turned to Alex. "Should we let them listen too?"

"Yes! Let them listen," Alex said with much importance, happy that somebody needed his permission.

"What would you say?" Papa turned to Jane.

Jane just nodded and said eagerly, "Papa, please hurry up and tell us! What happened to the cat?"

And Papa began his story. "You are not allowed to visit me very often. Even your letters rarely reach me—somehow they 'get lost' on the way. So, one time I happened to be feeling very homesick. I prayed to the Lord, because only to Him could I turn for comfort. Two days later one of the prisoners came up to me and said, 'Petrovich, I just had a visit with my wife. When it was over, the guards let me take some food to the barracks. I want to share it with you.' He handed me a small packet. As I unwrapped the paper, I saw a head of garlic and two figs. I thanked him—garlic in Siberian prison camp is such a valuable present!

"When I ate the figs, I decided not to throw away the pits. Instead I put them in an empty can and covered them with soil. I placed the can by the window and started watering them regularly. After a few weeks I noticed a green shoot; then a little palm leaf appeared! In summer we had a water shortage. Each prisoner was given only one tin of water per day, but I always shared my water ration with my plant. It was comforting to realize that my little palm tree needed me.

"And now I'll tell you about the cat. To this day I cannot imagine how that cat was able to get into our prison camp! Probably one of the guards secretly brought it in and then released it inside the camp. I was working the night shift as an electrician. One night I had some free time and decided to take a short walk in the prison yard. As I took the first few steps outside my shop, I was amazed to hear a mewing sound. The courtyard was brightly lit, and I noticed something dark against the wall. As I came closer I realized that it was a cat.

"I guessed that the cat was crying because of hunger. So I returned to the shop and found a small dish. Then I crumbled some bread from my ration and sprinkled it with water. As the cat started to devour the food, I noticed that she would soon have kittens. So I began feeding her on a regular basis. When the kittens were born, I started bringing the mother cat more food. As the kittens got bigger, the mother cat disappeared. I gave the kittens away to my friends in the barracks but decided to keep one tabby kitten. I called him Vaska.

"So, children, that's how I came to own a little palm tree and Vaska right here in the prison camp! The Lord answered my prayers and provided an unexpected joy. I even wrote a little poem about it for Jane and Alex. Do you want to hear it?"

"Yes, yes!" the kids shouted. "Please, Papa, read your poem!"

Papa began,

"I've shared a cup of water with a plant,
   My piece of bread I gave to a hungry kitten—"

"Papa, wait!" Alex interrupted. "Are you going to bring Vaska home with you when you are released?"

"We already have a cat!" Jane chimed in. "Alex named him Kisan. He and Vaska will be good friends; you'll see!"

"Unfortunately, kids, I won't come back home soon. My prison term ends in eight and a half years. You, Alex, will be twelve by then, and Jane will be nineteen! Imagine how grown up you will be! That's how long we'll have to wait for me to return home."

The next morning I woke up early. Papa and Lisa were already drinking tea in the kitchen and having a talk. I went back to the room so as not to disturb them. Such private times with Papa had become a special tradition during our visits to the camp. Papa would find time for a heart-to-heart talk with each of us. Lisa was already fifteen and had a lot to share with him.

After everyone was up, we had breakfast and began another happy day. But it ended sadly. In the evening our visit came to an abrupt ending. Because the time for our visit was scheduled to end the following morning, we had counted on spending another night with Papa. We had also planned to get up early the next day, have breakfast, pray together, and then say our good-byes.

But while we were eating supper there came a loud knock on the door. An officer came in and announced, "Vins, your visit is over! Some electrical equipment has broken down, and you will have to work the night shift."

"What if I go to work now," Papa tried to reason with him, "fix the problem, and return to my family for the rest of the night?"

"No, that's impossible!" the guard replied. "The camp administration gave a specific order to have you do the repairs. Get ready; I will be back in a few minutes!" And the officer left the room.

We began packing hurriedly. Alex and Jane were sobbing. Mama was also on the verge of tears. Papa tried to cheer us up. "Many unexpected things happen in life. This is just one of them. We must be thankful to God that we had almost two full days together. This has been such a holiday for me!"

Mama put a few heads of garlic in Papa's pocket. She wanted to add some candy, but Papa stopped her. "This is too much! I am not due for a relief package. I will be thankful if they let me keep the garlic!" As we prayed and hugged Papa good-bye, the guard opened the door. "Vins, time to go!" And he led Papa away.

We hurriedly finished packing our things. Mama was worried that it might already be too late to catch the last bus to Yakutsk. The officer came in, searched our bags, and handed us our passports. It was all over. And we stepped outside the prison gates into the cold winter night.

1

At the time I was about three, our family was small—just Papa, Mama, and me. We lived in downtown Kiev in a communal apartment with nine other families. Each family had one room. All neighbors shared one large kitchen. Our room was long and narrow, crowded with furniture. All our belongings were crammed up against the walls: my parents' bed, a dresser, a cupboard full of dishes, our dinner table, and the sofa that turned into my bed at night.

My favorite place in the room was a ceiling-high window with a wide sill. I liked to climb onto the sill, draw the curtain behind me, and watch the snowflakes whirl in the light of street lanterns, while the late pedestrians hurried somewhere and overcrowded buses pulled away from the bus stop.

In the morning it would still be dark outside when Mama woke me up, helped me get dressed, and took me to a daycare. Then my parents hurried off to work. Mama taught English in a high school, and Papa was an electrical engineer. After work Papa picked me up at the daycare. My favorite time of the day was after supper, when Mama would spread out her students' homework and begin grading it, while Papa and I sat cozily on our big sofa as he read children's books to me and told Bible stories.

When spring came and the days got longer, Papa often took me to a nearby park after supper. While I played with other children on the playground, he sat on a bench reading a magazine. One spring day Papa came to pick me up at daycare with a bicycle he had just bought for me—my very first one! After supper Papa adjusted the training wheels and we went to the park. That evening I learned to ride my new bike.

1

As my parents told me stories about God and taught me how to pray, I started telling Jesus all my childish needs. But when I was about five, the harmony of my small world was shattered by my kindergarten teacher. While telling us a story one day, she said that there was no God and that it was foolish to believe in Him.

I asked, "Why foolish? My Papa and Mama believe in God."

She laughed. "Natasha, God does not exist. Everyone knows that."

All the children laughed too, and I felt embarrassed to be so different from everyone else.

I often spent the weekends with Babushka, my grandmother. She lived on the outskirts of Kiev but worked downtown, not far from where we lived. In her late forties, young and merry, Babushka knew how to make wonderful games out of the simplest events in my childhood.

"Natasha, I bought you a great big doll for your birthday."

"Oh, hurry and show it to me!"

"No, my good girl. There are still two months before November 27. I left it in my desk at work till then."

"Well, does it close its eyes?"

"Absolutely! If you wish, I can describe to you what her hair is like, her dress, and the color of her eyes."

"Tell me."

As Babushka began describing the doll, it became real in my imagination. Together we chose a name for the new doll. As I counted the days till I would get to see it, the anticipation itself was a delight.

Often on the weekends Babushka took me to her house. We had to travel on the tram for over an hour. Babushka and I usually took a seat by the window, and right away I would start telling her about my friends in kindergarten, the games we played, and the new songs we learned. I even softly sang some for her right there on the tram. I also told her how the other children had laughed when I said that

my parents believed in God. She tried to explain why some people have different ideas about things.

After we arrived at her house and had lunch, we went to a park. At night before I went to bed she would tell me stories about Joseph and his evil brothers or about little Moses and what happened to him after the princess of Egypt rescued him from the river. I enjoyed my visits with Babushka a lot, but each time the weekend was over much too soon, and she had to take me back home.

In our overcrowded communal apartment, all the residents shared the main entrance, hallway, and kitchen. There was only one restroom for all ten families, so every morning neighbors were lined up outside the door, waiting for their turn. There were four gas stoves in the kitchen, and each family was allowed to use two burners. After preparing a meal, the housewife would carry the pots back to her family's room, where the family would eat. The kitchen was the liveliest place in the apartment as fresh gossip was discussed or squabbles erupted over burned kasha, boiled-over milk, or someone's using somebody else's burner.

When I was three and a half years old, my brother Peter was born. As Peter outgrew his crib and began to walk, Papa bought a folding cot. When it was set up at night, I could no longer get across to the window. My parents were on a waiting list for a two-room apartment. After they were told that they would have to wait ten more years for their turn to get an apartment, it was decided that the only solution was to remodel Babushka's attic, adding two bedrooms for us. Although Papa kept busy on this construction project each weekend and during summer vacations, it took him two years to finish the job.

On Sundays our family attended worship services at the Kiev Baptist Church. For Peter and me, Sundays were always special as we got up in the morning, put on our best clothes, and walked to the bus stop holding Papa's and Mama's hands. Other Christians would board our bus as we traveled. They would all smile, greet each other, and chat. When we reached the spacious church building with its pulpit and big piano, Papa, Mama, and Babushka would take their seats in the choir. I especially enjoyed services at Christmas and Easter. From our earliest childhood Peter and I enjoyed being in church.

2

When I was in the first grade, one evening Papa said to Peter and me, "Children, I have sad news. You will no longer be able to go to church with us. From now on, children are not allowed at the services. Mama and I will take turns staying at home with you on Sundays." Peter and I were sorry to hear this.

At school atheistic indoctrination had intensified after the first Soviet cosmonaut, Yuri Gagarin, flew into space in April of 1961. Mrs. Alekseeva, my first-grade teacher, told us all about his flight. She stressed how proud we should be that the first person in space was a Soviet man. Telling us about the scientific discoveries that resulted from his flight, she said, "The most important, children, is that Yuri Gagarin never saw in space any sort of God. He went up very high, as no one before him did, but he didn't see God or angels up there. That means there is no God! Remember this for the rest of your life."

As we approached the anniversary celebration of the Revolution, Mrs. Alekseeva began preparing us to join the "Octobrists," a communist organization for children. She held up a red star with a portrait of Lenin in the center and explained that each first grader would have a similar star pinned on his uniform in front of the school assembly.

"Children," she said, "this star is not just a simple badge. It must be worn only on the left side, over your heart. This means that now Lenin lives in your hearts!"

Mrs. Alekseeva read stories to us telling what a kind man Lenin was, how much he loved children, and what a wonderful life he had provided for all the people in the Soviet Union. But the teacher also told how much Lenin hated the Church and laughed at faith in God. I

was very puzzled by all this as I tried to figure out why at home I was told that believing in God was good and honorable, while at school I heard just the opposite.

However, I trusted my parents implicitly, and if they believed that God existed, then it must be true. No doubts arose as I prayed and loved Jesus in a childlike way. What troubled me was that my teacher might find out that I was from a Christian family. The thought of her announcing it in class was terrifying. On the appointed day I joined the "Octobrists" along with the rest of my classmates.

That year my little sister Lisa was born. Now there were five of us crowded into one room, and Papa hurried with the construction so that we could move into Babushka's house as soon as possible. When I was in second grade, we finally moved there.

One summer evening, Babushka called Peter and me away from our play and told us to wash up and get ready for bed. Her words drew a storm of protests. "Why must we go to bed so early? It is not even dark yet!"

But Babushka said, "Tomorrow, early in the morning, we are all going to a church service."

Peter and I could not believe what we heard. "But children aren't allowed at the services! Did you forget, Babushka?"

"No, I did not forget. But things have changed, and now you can come to church with us. So, hurry up and get ready for bed."

The next day we awoke to a bright Sunday morning, had breakfast, and set out for church. We traveled for two hours by bus, tram, and lastly commuter train. At last the train stopped at a small station in the woods. About thirty other people got off with us, and we all started down a pathway into the woods.

As we walked I tugged at Babushka's hand. "Where are we going? This is not the way to church!"

"Just wait." she answered without stopping. "Soon you will see for yourself."

At last we reached a large meadow. Everyone began spreading blankets on the grass and taking a seat. I still did not understand what was happening. "Babushka, is the service going to be right here? But where is the church building? Where is the pulpit?"

Babushka smiled, "This is our new place for Sunday services. Don't you like it? Look, the trees surround us like walls, and the sky is our ceiling. The sun is shining, birds are singing—don't you like it?"

I looked around. "Yes, it's nice, . . . but is this really a church?"

Just then one of the men standing in the middle asked everyone to bow his head for prayer. From that moment on the familiar atmosphere of Sunday worship surrounded me—hymns, sermons, prayers. One of the preachers was my papa.

Many changes took place for Peter and me after that first worship service in the woods. Papa explained to us, "The police might come to one of our meetings, arrest me, and take me to prison because I preach from the Bible. Mama, Babushka, and I realize all this, but we have decided to join the persecuted church."

He also said that difficulties might come not just for the grownups in our family, but also for me in school. "You are already nine, Natasha, and can understand a great deal. For many months you and Peter couldn't go to church, because children were forbidden at the worship services. Unfortunately, these regulations were made by church leaders who gave in to pressure from the atheistic authorities. But when the church submits to such unbiblical demands, it disobeys the Lord's commandments. There are many other things going on that have forced us to start a new church. But you are still too young to understand it all. Just remember the most important thing—your parents love Jesus and want to live according to the Bible."

That is how our carefree childhood abruptly ended: for me at the age of nine; for Peter at six; and little Lisa was not even big enough to remember the days when Papa spent his evenings at home, reading us children's books and taking us to the playground in the park. Our family entered a harsh period of persecution that was to last several decades.

3

In October of 1962, a long article criticizing Christians appeared in the *Evening Kiev* newspaper. My parents' names were mentioned in it. The next day at school, my teacher Mrs. Alekseeva was telling us about cavemen, their customs, and religious practices. Suddenly she exclaimed, "Children, can you imagine that even in our day there are people who believe in God just like those cavemen did?"

The kids giggled. "Science has proven that there is no God," the teacher continued, "and progressive-minded mankind rejected all religious beliefs long ago. But occasionally even today we encounter people stupefied by religion. And such a girl is in our own class!" Mrs. Alekseeva stopped and peered at the class.

Everyone was silent, waiting for what would come next. She turned to me. "Natasha Vins, come forward, stand before the class, and tell your comrades. Is it true that you believe in God?" I felt a sudden panic. Like a little animal being hunted, I wanted to hide, to become invisible.

"Well? How long do we have to wait?" the teacher repeated in a stern voice.

Slowly I walked forward and turned to face the class. Tense silence hung in the air. Quietly, almost in a whisper, I said, "Yes, I believe in God."

"What's wrong with you?" the teacher exclaimed angrily. "Are you that ignorant? Didn't you read what Yuri Gagarin said after he returned from his space flight? It was in all the newspapers. He did not see God anywhere! You're in the third grade already! The Soviet State is making every effort to give its children the best education in the world, and here is the result. How shameful! Go to the principal's office. Galina Kirilovna wants to talk to you!"

I left the classroom and made my way down the hall to the principal's office. I was scared. Only the worst behaved boys were ever sent to the principal, never girls. I was the first one. What would the principal say to me? How should I answer? As Babushka had taught me, I prayed silently, "Jesus, help me. Teach me what to do." And I knocked on the principal's door.

"Come in!" called the no-nonsense voice of Galina Kirilovna. I entered. She was not alone in the office. Her assistant Valentina Anatolievna was also present. The principal looked sternly at me. "Are you Natasha Vins? Come in. Sit in this chair. I want to talk to you about the article in the *Evening Kiev*. Do your parents subscribe to it? Did they read yesterday's paper?"

"Yes."

"So, is it true that your parents are sectarians?"

"Papa and Mama are Christians."

"How about you? Do you also believe in God?"

"Yes."

"Just look at her, Valentina Anatolievna! At nine years of age she is already a confirmed sectarian. Natasha, our school will not tolerate this. We will make you change your mind. Valentina Anatolievna will give you atheistic instruction. That's all for now. You may go back to your classroom."

I left the office. Recess had already started, and the halls were bubbling with life. I stood by a window. How could I go back to class? What would my classmates think after everything that the teacher had said about me? And now on top of everything else was this call to the principal's office! What would my friend Tanya think? We shared a desk, but would she even talk to me now?

I knew that I could not stand by the hall window all day. So I reluctantly walked toward my classroom. As I entered, I immediately felt that things would never be the same. My classmates had discovered that I was strikingly different from everyone else, and our relationships changed. In our class of thirty kids I was the only one from a Christian family. That day, at the age of nine, I became an outcast among the children.

At home I told Babushka what had happened at school. She was very concerned and questioned me about every detail. Finally she said, "You are forced quite early in life to pay the price for your faith in God. It is not a simple matter. I know from experience. Your grandfather was killed in prison for his Christian faith. Your Papa also had a difficult childhood, and now it's your turn. But don't lose heart. You'll make it with God's help. And your family will always stand by you." Babushka suggested that we pray, and as we did, the fear loosened its grip on my heart.

As a result of the article in the *Evening Kiev*, Mama lost her job. Papa was demoted from his position as the department head to an ordinary engineer with less pay and responsibility. At school I was summoned twice a week to Valentina Anatolievna's office for "atheistic instruction." She was extremely quick-tempered. Each time she was dissatisfied with my reply to a question, she would shout at me. At first, I was frightened each time I was called to her office, but as time went on, I grew accustomed to these "discussions" and her shouting.

The annual celebration of the Revolution, observed each November, was nearing again. Our teacher announced that the most outstanding students from our class were to become Young Pioneers that day. She explained that next spring on May 1, the whole class would join the Pioneers, but at present only ten of us would be chosen. "Children," she said, "it's a great honor to be selected to join the Young Pioneers first. Think it over carefully, and name only the most worthy among you."

Names were called out and, to my surprise, I was named too. I could not believe it! How could I possibly be considered worthy, since the teacher had often announced before the class that I brought shame to the entire school? To my amazement, the teacher enthusiastically supported my candidacy. "That's right, children! When Natasha steps into the ranks of the Young Pioneers, she will not dare to shame her red tie and will have to reject her religious prejudices. Let's vote for her!"

I was elected unanimously. Mrs. Alekseeva turned to me. "Natasha, the class has shown you great honor in choosing you to be among our first Young Pioneers. Now, children, who else shall we elect?"

I raised my hand. She asked, "Natasha, who would you like to name as a candidate?"

Standing at my desk, I quietly said, "Mrs. Alekseeva, I cannot join the Pioneers."

"Do you realize what you're saying?" the teacher shouted. "This is an insult to the entire class! Your comrades decided to place their trust in you despite your sectarian background. And you reject it? You just spit on all this?"

She ran out of words and just stared at me. I remained standing beside my desk. Everyone's head was turned my way. At last the teacher questioned, "All right, tell me why you can't be a Pioneer."

"When you read us the constitution of the Young Pioneers, it said that every Pioneer must actively fight against religion. I can't do this because I am a Christian."

"That's enough!" She interrupted. "We've heard from you more than once that you're a Christian. So, you're refusing to join the Pioneers? Did you hear that, kids?"

The class buzzed excitedly. Mrs. Alekseeva continued, "Do you realize that you undermine the reputation of our class? Don't you care that from now on we will take last place in all our school's competitions? Only because of your stupid stubbornness! Believe me, sooner or later you will realize that there is no God and that only uneducated old people need religion."

The bell rang for recess, and the teacher left the classroom. The children gathered around my desk. Everyone was flustered and angry, especially the boys. They all shouted, interrupting one another. Someone pulled on my braid, and I began to cry. "Crybaby. Just wait till classes are over and we go outside! There'll be something else for you to cry about! We'll show you how we treat people who bring shame on our class."

4

Home became the only place where I felt secure. It was a struggle to go back to school every day. Mama met with my teacher and the principal. She tried to reason with them. She asked them to stop pressuring me and simply accept me as I was—a little girl from a Christian home. But they replied with indignation, accusing her of being a mother who "cripples the life of her own child."

One December evening, while our family was eating supper, a committee composed of my teacher, the principal's assistant, and a city official appeared at our home. They arrived unannounced and after introducing themselves gave the reason for their visit. Apparently the principal's assistant, after several sessions with me, had sent a report to the regional office stating, "Natasha Vins is not responding to re-education, and the school requests that city officials take appropriate action."

As a result, a court case was opened to deprive my parents of their parental rights. The committee had come to examine our living conditions and to issue one last warning. They emphasized that not only would I be placed in an orphanage, but Peter and Lisa would be taken away as well.

After our visitors left, we were overwhelmed with grief. Only two-year-old Lisa did not understand what was going on. Papa took Peter and me in his arms to comfort us. Our family knelt and prayed together, children and adults, asking for God's protection. Our parents tried not to show their worry, understanding how traumatic all this was for us children.

Babushka immediately began talking in a practical way. "Natasha, Peter, we must be prepared for this. Usually in such cases, the children are taken and placed in an orphanage somewhere in a remote town. The officials' strategy is to hide children to keep their parents from visiting them. Brothers and sisters from the same Christian family are never placed together. Even if you were able to send a letter home, we would not receive it, since the mail addressed to us will be checked by the KGB. You will have to memorize the address of Emma [an elderly Jewish lady who had once been our neighbor]. As soon as you have the chance to let us know where you are, send a note to her address. We will warn her to bring it to us right away."

It took me a long time to get to sleep that night. I kept thinking, "What will happen to me now? What's life in an orphanage like? How will I ever live without Mama, Papa, and Babushka? Without Peter and Lisa?"

The next day, Valentina Anatolievna called me into her office. "Natasha, did your parents tell you why we came to your house yesterday?"

"Yes, Valentina Anatolievna."

"Well, you know, if you become a Young Pioneer, you will remain at home with your parents and little brother and sister. Perhaps it's your parents who won't allow you to join the Pioneers? But why do you have to tell them? Let's keep it a secret. You may wear your red tie during the day in school and leave it in your teacher's desk before going home. Go back to class and think this over carefully."

I returned to the classroom and sat down at my desk. The teacher was explaining some grammar rules, but it was impossible for me to concentrate. I could only think of my own problems. "What should I do now? I refused to join the Pioneers on my own, not because my parents forbade it. Of course, they would be disappointed if I joined, but they would not try to stop me. I myself don't wish to do it! How can I believe in God and at the same time join the Pioneers, promising to fight against religion? I can't do that!"

The winter break began with sledding, skiing, and preparations for Christmas. We put up a Christmas tree. Mama and Babushka were busy cooking and baking for the holidays. Our home was filled with the aroma of Christmas cookies. Babushka checked every day to see how well Peter and I had memorized our passages from the second chapter of Luke for the children's program to be held in another home in Kiev. In all the holiday happiness, my school troubles were completely forgotten.

The children's Christmas program lasted several hours. In a spacious room emptied of furniture stood a tall Christmas tree decorated with lights and ornaments. Paper snowflakes were suspended from the ceiling, and the Bethlehem star shone brightly in a corner. For me the greatest excitement was to see all these Christian children! At school I always felt so different from the rest of the kids since I was the only Christian in my class. But here, at the Christmas program, everywhere I turned there were Christian kids!

Together we sang "Silent Night," and children recited various Christmas poems. Peter and I also quoted the story about Jesus' birth from the Gospel of Luke. At the close of the celebration every child was given a gift of cookies and candy.

When the Christmas program was over and we were putting our coats on, a young lady who had played the guitar while the children sang, walked up to me. Masha was twenty years old and looked so beautiful and kind. "Natasha," she said, "on Tuesday evening at six o'clock your children's Sunday school class will have its first meeting. I will be your teacher. Please come."

That Tuesday evening, about fifteen of us gathered in Alex's apartment. I remembered Alex from our Christmas program; he was a year older than I. Alex's mother met us at the door, took our coats and hats, and led us into the room. When everyone had arrived, Masha picked up her guitar and we sang several children's songs. Then she began a lesson on how God created the world in which we live. She read from Genesis chapter one, explained it, and asked us questions. At first we were shy because we did not know each other very well. But little by little this passed, and we had a lively time discussing Creation.

At the end Masha said, "Now we will pray, but before we do I want to say something. Your teachers at school are atheists. They try to convince you that there is no God. Perhaps they ask you questions about God's existence that you can't answer. Let's talk about this at the beginning of our next meeting and together we'll try to find answers for your teachers' tough questions." As we were dismissed, Masha warned us, "When you go out, try to be very quiet. Don't all leave at the same time. We must be careful so that the KGB will not find out about our meetings."

Another school semester began, and once again came the summons to Valentina Anatolievna's office. Now she added threats of the approaching court case that would place me in an orphanage. After those sessions I would return home in tears. My parents decided to write a petition and send it to various government departments requesting that the harassment of our family be stopped. They also let Christians in other towns know what was happening so that they could pray earnestly for us.

To me Babushka said, "Don't you worry! The Lord will help and protect you. But even if the court case proceeds and you are taken away, send your new address to Emma. I will travel to that city and ask for work in your orphanage as a cleaning lady. You and I will not admit to anyone that we know each other. But when nobody is around as you walk past me in the hall where I am mopping the floor, we will smile at each other, or maybe even have a chance to exchange a few words." This conversation cheered me up, and I no longer felt so sad.

At the next children's meeting, just as Masha promised, we discussed our school problems. Alex told how his teacher insisted he join the Pioneers and often kept him after school because he would not give in to her demands. One time the teacher said to him, "Alex, stop being so stubborn! Perhaps your mother won't give you the money for a red tie? Just ask, and the school will provide one."

"No, money is not a problem." Alex answered.

She kept insisting. Finally Alex said, "All right, I'll bring a tie to-morrow!"

The teacher beamed and let him go home. The next day she came up to his desk. "Alex, did you bring the tie?" Alex opened his school bag and pulled out his father's Sunday tie. The teacher began shouting at him, "What a liar!"

But Alex replied, "I agreed yesterday to bring a tie to school, but I never promised you it would be the red Pioneers' tie."

We all laughed so hard when Alex told his story that Masha had a hard time getting us to quiet down. The next person to tell about her school problems was Lena. In her class the teacher spoke about Yuri Gagarin's space flight and how he did not see God when he was in outer space. Then the teacher turned to Lena, "You tell us that God exists. So why didn't Yuri Gagarin see Him?"

Lena answered, "It is written in the Bible that only the pure in heart will see God. Probably his heart was not pure."

All the children had something to share. I also told about my difficulties at school and the threat to send me to an orphanage. At the close of the meeting we all got on our knees and prayed for one another. During this time of sharing and praying, it seemed to me that I had grown wings! I felt that I was not "the only strange child among hundreds of normal kids," as my teacher would often say. All the children in this room believed in God the same way I did! The beginning of weekly children's meetings opened a bright new page in my life.

5

One Sunday in the spring of 1963, as the worship service was drawing to a close, policemen appeared from behind the trees. They surrounded us, shouting, "Halt this meeting! Disperse! This is an illegal meeting!" Their leader, a major, began pushing his way into the middle of the gathering. The choir continued singing a hymn. One of the preachers approached the major and asked him not to disrupt the service. But the officer pushed him aside and barked an order to another policeman to arrest him. Christians surrounded the choir and the preachers in a tight circle, attempting to prevent their arrest. The police became violent.

At home, Papa explained to Peter and me what to do if we were ever taken to the police station and interrogated. He told us not to be afraid, but to remember not to mention any believers' names during the questioning because those people might be arrested as a result. "For instance," he said, "if they ask you who teaches Bible lessons at the children's meetings and you name Masha or Vera, they could be arrested and get several years in prison. So when you are questioned about church matters, it is best not to answer at all. Be silent just as Jesus was when Pilate interrogated Him."

From that time on, the locations for worship services were arranged very carefully. Only two or three people would know ahead of time where the Sunday service would be held. Everyone else would come to a bus stop at an appointed time and receive instructions where to go next. Several Sundays passed peacefully. But in June the police raided another service, where about 150 believers were present. During the closing prayer, policemen rushed at us. They began to drag and shove people, trying to force their way into the middle of the circle where the preachers stood. Peter and I were very frightened. We clung to Babushka as she tried to comfort us. We were concerned for Papa because he was in the middle where the most vigorous assault was taking place. (Mama had stayed home with little Lisa that day.)

Nineteen people were arrested and sentenced to fifteen days in jail, including Papa. During the interrogations, he was informed that a criminal case was being initiated against him. They told him that if he were arrested again, he would not get off so easily. When Papa returned to work after fifteen days in jail, he was asked to hand in his resignation.

Another long article blaming Christians was published in the *Evening Kiev*, describing the service the police had broken up. When the new school year began in September, I was faced with even more opposition than the year before. That fall Peter had to start first grade. Our parents decided to place him in a different school because the administration at my school was extremely negative toward Christians.

That fall we also parted with Papa. Because his arrest and long imprisonment were inevitable in Kiev, our church's ministers suggested that he leave home and live in hiding in the houses of believers in different towns. This would give him ministry opportunities in churches all over the country and also help him to avoid arrest. Our church resolved to provide monthly support for our family.

Peter and I experienced many firsts during those years: the first meetings in the forest, the first secret Sunday school, the first disruption of services by the police. And our first house search. In the years to come, the police and KGB stormed into our home many times, turning everything upside down. But we remember most vividly the first search that took place when we were still little.

It happened late at night when we were already asleep. The doorbell rang, and we heard a loud banging on the door. "Open up! Police!" About fifteen men, some uniformed policemen and other KGB officers in civilian clothes, stormed into our house. As I awoke from the noise downstairs, Babushka bent over me and whispered hurriedly,

"A search! Try not to get up! Save our Bible!" And she shoved our family Bible under my mattress.

The boots of the police stomped up the stairs, which led to the bedroom where we children slept. Two-year-old Lisa began to cry, and Babushka went to her bed. I had a terrifying thought: "What if the police find the Bible under my mattress? What will they do to me then?"

The first policeman entered our bedroom and flicked on the light. Two more were trailing behind him. Babushka protested. "What are you doing? Why do you have to wake the children up? You could just turn on the table lamp!"

The policeman answered gruffly, "I know what I am doing!"

Peter sat up in bed, rubbing his eyes sleepily. Lisa sobbed as Babushka held her. I lay still and looked at the policemen with fright.

The search lasted for several hours. Every room was ransacked. Clothing and bedding from the shelves were thrown onto the floor. In the kitchen, they sifted the flour, cereal, and sugar, and peered into each pot and pan. For some reason they even took the iron apart. Of course, they ordered me out of bed and found the Bible under my mattress.

They were particularly interested in books, turning pages one by one, looking for notes or papers between the pages. They even carefully examined Peter's and my school notebooks and textbooks. All our family photographs, personal letters, addresses of relatives, our Bible, and a hymnbook were placed on the dinner table, where one of the state officials made a list of all the items they were going to confiscate. It was almost dawn when they left.

At school, preparations for the anniversary of the Revolution began that year well in advance. Our class was assigned to do reports on the lives of Young Pioneer heroes. Mrs. Alekseeva announced that the best report would be read in front of the school assembly. She handed us assignments, and I ended up with Pavlik Morozov.

I knew his story well. Pavlik informed the police that his father had hidden a portion of his own crop before all the grain was taken from peasants by the collective farm. Thirteen-year-old Pavlik showed the police where the grain was hidden, and they confiscated it. Pavlik's father, who had hidden the grain to protect his family from starvation, was arrested. A few days later a neighbor killed Pavlik for betraying his father.

Our textbooks portrayed Pavlik as a hero and his act of reporting on his father as an example to be imitated. I knew why the teacher had assigned me this story. If I wrote that Pavlik's example was one we all should follow, then I would be expected to report on my own father. But to betray Papa was unthinkable! I did not approve of Pavlik Morozov's act, even though I felt sorry for him that he was killed. But I could never call him my hero.

What should I do? I could not write the report the way my teacher expected me to. If I totally refused to do it, the outcome might be much more serious than just the low grade. I came home from school feeling discouraged and asked Babushka's advice. She agreed with me that I could not do the report. She suggested that I tell my teacher that since I was not a Pioneer myself, it would not be proper for me to do a report on a Young Pioneer hero. I agreed but was nervous about the reaction of my teacher and classmates.

The next day I told the teacher why I could not do the report. She became very angry. After class began, she announced, "Natasha Vins has let you all down again! But what's even more terrible, she has shown disrespect to the memory of Pavlik Morozov, who died as a hero serving the cause of the Soviet State!"

The reaction of my classmates was extremely negative. No one would speak to me during recess, not even Tanya. I felt terribly alone, but knew I could not act against my conscience. While walking home after school, some boys from class attacked me and beat me up. Babushka decided that this situation could not continue like this and went to school with me the next morning.

At that time much was written in the Soviet newspapers about the lack of civil rights for blacks in the United States. One article told of a boy who was not permitted to ride the school bus with white children. His parents intervened for him with the school administration and were successful. But then white children started beating him up.

As a result, a policeman was assigned to accompany the black boy to school. The Soviet papers expressed great shock over such terrible discrimination against the rights of blacks in the United States.

Babushka took this article with her when she went to talk to my principal. During their discussion she stated, "I will not permit such humiliations against Natasha to continue. I am convinced that the children ridiculed her and beat her up because of what the teacher said in class. Just look at this article! Do you realize that the discrimination experienced by a child from a Christian family in a Soviet school is quite similar to the discrimination against blacks in the United States? Unless I hear from you today that you guarantee Natasha's safety at school, I will be forced to demand that a policeman accompany her to school, just like that black boy in America."

The principal agreed to look into this problem and somehow resolve it. As a result of Babushka's visit with the principal, I was left alone for a while.

# 6

In March of 1965, a new little sister was born into our family. She was named Jane. Papa was still in hiding, coming to Kiev on rare occasions to meet with Mama and us in the homes of relatives. The secret police continued to keep our house under surveillance. When Jane was born, Papa longed to see his newest baby. Very late one night he came home, taking a great risk. We were all happy to see him, but understood that we must be careful not to tell any outsider that Papa was home. If someone rang the doorbell, Papa went into the bedroom so he would not be seen. He stayed home for two days. The Lord protected us from danger, and we had a wonderful time together.

Another year passed, and in May of 1966 I was already finishing the sixth grade and Peter the third. The situation at school had improved. For some reason, the threat of being taken away from our parents and placed in an orphanage was no longer mentioned. One day I came home from school and could tell by Mama and Babushka's faces that something was terribly wrong. A friend from Moscow had brought the news that Papa had been arrested two days earlier. Even though he had already been in hiding for three years and we had known that he could be arrested at any moment, this news was sudden and brought a stab of pain.

As soon as I heard the news, I went to my room and shut the door. I looked at his picture wondering, "Where is Papa now? Is he alone in his cell? Or being questioned by an investigator? Is he in danger? When will I see him again?" Mama called me downstairs for dinner, but I did not feel like eating.

The next day, our Sunday worship service in the forest was brutally disrupted. Policemen beat the men and twisted their arms. They pushed around women and children. With my own eyes, I saw seventy-five-year old Fanya Andreevna get shoved so hard that her cane went flying to the side and she fell down. I ran to help her get up, but she could not because she was badly injured. Many believers were arrested that day and sentenced to fifteen days in jail.

At our home the police conducted another house search. They officially informed us that Papa had been arrested and that while his case was being prepared for trial he would be held in Lefortovo Prison in Moscow. The prosecutor in Moscow assigned an investigator in Kiev to question family members.

One day at Peter's school his third-grade teacher was told to send him to the principal's office. Peter figured out that he was going to be interrogated. So instead of going to the principal's office, he ran out of school, got on a bus, and went to the home of relatives who lived across town. Mama happened to be there and decided not to bring Peter home, but to send him to a village to stay with a Christian family in order to protect him from interrogation.

I did not succeed in evading interrogation. When the investigator came to my school, the teacher personally took me to the principal's office. The investigator started to question me about Papa, but I refused to answer his questions. He got angry and shouted at me as did the principal, but they were unable to get any information from me.

Later Papa told us how in the Lefortovo Prison he was reading the reports of Kiev's investigator and came across this statement: "I tried to question Natasha Vins, but she refused to answer any questions. Peter Vins ran away from school, and I was unable to locate him all summer long." Papa smiled as he read these reports.

Papa spent six months in prison before his trial. During that time, no visits or correspondence with him were permitted. The date of the trial was kept secret from our family. In order to be there when the trial would take place, Mama and Babushka traveled to Moscow in advance and stayed with relatives, checking the court schedules every day. Six-year-old Lisa went with them, while Peter and I stayed home in order not to miss school. An elderly Christian woman agreed to take care of little Jane and us.

Several weeks went by till at last the telegram came from Moscow, "The trial has started; bring the children immediately." That same evening Masha took us to the train station, and by morning we were in Moscow. At the courthouse we arrived during a recess. About forty Christians were standing in the hall, with Mama and Babushka among them. They were happy to see us. Mama wanted to know all about little Jane back home.

Suddenly, at the far end of the corridor we saw the guards coming in our direction. Babushka quickly drew Peter and me to the front of the crowd, saying, "Look quickly! There is Papa!" When Papa saw us he smiled and waved at us. But all this lasted less than a minute as he was led into the courtroom.

Most of the Christians who showed up were not allowed in the courtroom and remained in the corridor. Only relatives of the accused and a few others were able to be present at the trial. Since Peter and I were underage, we were told to stay in the corridor. Throughout the day there were several breaks. The accused were led out and then back into the courtroom, and each time Peter and I would see Papa for a brief moment. Late in the evening the trial ended. Both Papa and Pastor Kryuchkov were sentenced to three years in prison camps.

The next day we went to see Papa at Lefortovo Prison. All five of us—Mama, Babushka, Peter, Lisa, and I—were allowed in. At the prison entrance the guards checked our passports and birth certificates. Mama showed the notice from the judge allowing us a visit. All the documents were in order, so we were permitted to enter.

A guard led us into a large room that had no other furniture except for a table and several chairs. He ordered us to sit on one side of the table. The chair reserved for Papa was on the opposite side. An officer sat at the far end of the table. He announced that we were allowed a thirty-minute visit and that he would be present the whole time. He also told us that the visit would end if we asked Papa inappropriate questions about prison conditions.

A young guard led Papa in. For the first time in many months we saw him up close. Peter touched his hand and exclaimed, "Oh, Papa, your hands are so cold! Is your prison cell—"

"I have already warned you not to discuss the conditions in the cell!" the officer interrupted him. "Don't you understand that?"

We were frozen with fear that this man might cut our visit short. Babushka hurried to explain. "Please excuse him! Peter is only ten and just didn't think before he spoke."

The officer nodded without saying a word. The visit was allowed to proceed, and we continued talking. All of a sudden Lisa started to sing a hymn. We were alarmed. What if this would end our visit? But the officer himself watched in amazement as the six-year-old, in her innocent childish voice, sang glory to God in prison. With tears in his eyes Papa hugged his courageous little girl and said quietly, "Thank you, my dear!"

As the visit drew to an end, Papa said to the officer, "Please, let us pray together." The officer shrugged his shoulders unobligingly. We bowed our heads, and Papa prayed.

As we said our last good-byes, the guard entered, announcing, "It's over. Time to leave!"

We left the prison gates and walked to the bus stop through the snowy streets of Moscow. The day was December 2, 1966. We had to get to the train station and return home to Kiev. There was nothing left to be done that would keep us in Moscow. As for Papa, he would soon be on his way to a prison camp in the Ural Mountains.

7

From Moscow, Papa and the other prisoners were transported under guard to a prison camp in the Ural Mountains. They were in transit for over three weeks. As soon as Papa let us know his new address, Mama started packing and went to visit him. It was a long trip. First she had to ride an overnight train from Kiev to Moscow. Next she had to change trains and travel for two more days to Solikamsk. From there she flew on a small ten-seat airplane to a town called Chepets. Finally, at the end of this long and exhausting journey, she arrived at the camp and was allowed a brief visit with Papa. She also was able to leave him some food and warm clothes.

Because visits with Papa were permitted only a few times a year, letters became the main link between us. However, we had to be very careful with our letters because the prison camp censors checked them. Often letters from Papa were "lost" along the way. But those that reached us brought much-awaited news that he was well.

His letters helped us get a glimpse of his life in a prison camp in the midst of forests and swamps. Papa's new poems revealed what was on his heart during the lonely evenings in the overcrowded, noisy barracks or trudging over snow-covered forest trails as the guards with their watchdogs led the prisoners to the logging site.

But for us children, the most significant message in his letters was that each of us was special to him. We felt it was important for Papa to know what was happening in our lives. Here is an excerpt from his letter to Peter:

April 1, 1967

My dear son,

I read your letter with much interest. I am very glad about your progress in school and in your music lessons. Babushka wrote me that you are very helpful around the house, especially in shoveling all that snow. I am so glad that you are growing up to be such a diligent, hardworking boy. Soon you will turn eleven. I want to wish you a very happy birthday, my dear boy!

In his letter to me, Papa wrote:

February 15, 1968

Dear Natasha, my precious firstborn,

I received your letter of January 9th. I did as you asked me and said hello from you to the taiga and the mountains. I am so glad that you deeply love your homeland and its people. Living for the good of others is a noble goal that makes life meaningful. That is how our Lord Jesus Christ lived on earth, and also many men and women of faith, including your grandfather Peter.

Did you get my letter with the new Christmas poem? Please let me know. Give my greetings to Babushka, Mama, Peter, Lisa, and Jane.

Your Papa

In his letter to Mama, Papa wrote:

October 5, 1968

Nadia, my dearest,

I greet and hug you! How are you managing with the children all by yourself? I am constantly thinking about you. I always pray for you, the children, and our dear Babushka. Thank you for the family picture: the children are growing up, while you and I are getting older. Our hair is getting gray, and all this while we have been apart for years . . . But don't be discouraged: the Lord is with us! It is most important that we remain faithful to Him and to each other in sincere love. May the Lord protect you all. I am praying for a chance to see you. Please read 2 Cor. 1:3–10 (especially verses 3, 4, 5).

With much love,

Your Georgi

We always eagerly awaited Papa's letters, especially before our birthdays and Christmas. When a letter from him would finally arrive in our mailbox, we all gathered around the table or the shining Christmas tree and read it out loud.

December 10, 1967

My dear children, Nadia, Mama,

I want to wish you all Merry Christmas! From my early childhood Christmas stays in my memory, filled with joyful family celebration, Christmas carols, and a wonderful Bible story about the birth of the Savior. I wish I could share the happiness of this holiday with you, my dear ones. But this is the second year I have to celebrate this day by myself: last year behind bars in Lefortovo Prison, and now in a faraway prison camp, lost in the forests of the Ural Mountains . . .

My children, this Christmas Eve tune your radio to a Christian station and join your voices in singing the wonderful melody of "Silent Night." At this hour I will also, being far away from you, unite my voice with yours, singing: "Christ the Savior is born!"

I recently had a chance to read a book by Rudolf Bershadski, *The Other Parts of the World,* in which he describes a moving scene on the central square of Wellington, New Zealand, on Christmas Day, where a big children's choir was singing "Silent Night." The author describes how deeply he was moved—he, who was raised in an atheistic society—as he gazed into the glowing faces of children praising God's Son. He exclaims, "You should have seen the faces of those singing children!" He goes on to describe how all the adults who filled the town square took their hats off in respect for the event . . .

From Papa's letters we found out about the important moments in his prison life:

July 20, 1967

My dear ones,

Because of God's mercies I am still alive and continue my path in bonds. I work on the same work crew, doing the same job. At the beginning of December, a committee from Moscow came to our camp to consider prisoners for an amnesty in commemoration of the fiftieth anniversary of the Revolution (1917–67). I, too, was summoned to stand before the committee. They demanded that I acknowledge that I was guilty of a crime, which I could not agree to since there was no crime in my Christian activities. After a short discussion the head of the committee announced that I was denied amnesty.

As a result of the amnesty, many prisoners were released; others had their terms cut in half. I was happy for them and only hope that as they are freed they will not return to their old crimes. As I observed their faces transformed with happiness and anticipation over their imminent release, it was painful to think that I was denied freedom because of my Christian stand. Then a thought crossed my mind: how did Christ feel when Barabbas was freed instead of Him? And Jesus had to die on the cross for him too—for the criminal. Looking at Christ gives me strength and courage in my chosen path . . .

Here is another excerpt from Papa's letters to me:

November 28, 1968

Dear Natasha,

Yesterday, on November 27, you were in my prayers all day. I hug you and wish you a Happy Birthday! May the Lord protect you in His love. I remember the days when you were a tiny baby, and then your first steps, first words . . . You are my first song, my firstborn!

I have a request for you. I read in a newspaper that the Postal Service has printed a series of postage stamps in recognition of the artistry of the Dutch painter Rembrandt. This series will include his works "David and Jonathan," "The Parable of the Vineyard," and others. Try to buy two or three sets at the post office or at the stamp collector's store, and send me one.

Give my greetings to everyone at home. I hug and kiss you.

Your Papa

Babushka's first letter to Papa, after he had been moved from the Moscow prison to the northern Urals, was one of a handful of letters that survived numerous house searches.

May 19, 1967

Dear Georgi!

I received your first letter from the camp, and it was a comfort to me. Today is the sad and painful anniversary of your arrest. But take courage, don't let your heart be downcast. On that day you acted honorably, worthy of your father. May the Lord remove all heaviness from your heart.

28

I would like to tell you about our sorrows and joys, but not now. So far everything is fine. The trees in our yard are in bloom, the days are flying quickly, and our lives are flying with them. But the important truth is that "their works do follow them." Every person is destined to live on earth for only a short time. What matters is how one lives his days.

The path of honesty is difficult. I do not mean honesty in financial matters only, but rather spiritual honesty, not compromising one's convictions for personal gain. Many have traveled their life's journey with such high Christian integrity, but in comparison with the general masses they are just a few. In most cases, they were admired only after they died, while during their lifetime people considered them peculiar and strange. The motto of our day is to squeeze everything out of life for personal gain. But how often such people, like butterflies, quickly burn their wings in the fire of life and crawl defeated and empty-hearted for the rest of their days.

Your path is difficult. I know that you have times of loneliness, when you feel you could fall down under the heaviness of your cross. Do not despair even then, but remember that the sun is always shining behind the cloud! You are still young, and Lord willing, will live through it and even forget these hardships. Only valuable lessons learned in prison will remain with you for the rest of your life.

Dear Georgi, take courage! You will not even notice how fast the years of imprisonment will fly by and your term will be over. You will come home to us and once again experience the joy of freedom. May God protect you! Let's put our trust in Him, because our breath and life are in His hands.

Your Mama

8

When Papa was arrested in May of 1966, Babushka was sixty years old and had already retired. She immediately traveled to Moscow to meet with the prosecutor and find out what her son was accused of. She also took Papa a relief package. On that trip Babushka met wives and mothers of Christian prisoners from different cities who came to Moscow to find out what they could do for their loved ones awaiting trial in Lefortovo Prison.

While in Moscow, many of them stayed in the home of an elderly preacher, Afanasy Yakimenko, on the outskirts of the city. At the end of each day, exhausted and overwhelmed after spending long hours at the prosecutor's office or by the prison entrance to hand over food packages, they would return to Yakimenko's house. As they ate supper, each one would share the events of her day. They prayed together and looked for comfort in God's Word. Babushka recalled later what an encouragement such fellowship was for each of them.

In June of that year, over twenty wives and mothers of prisoners gathered in Moscow from Siberia, Central Asia, Ukraine, Belorussia, and Moldavia. This was the first conference of the reorganized Council of Prisoners' Relatives.* They spent time in prayer and discussion, searching for the best ways to help the prisoners. They decided to keep a detailed file on each Baptist believer arrested for Christian activities

---

*The Council of Prisoners' Relatives was first organized in 1964, when numerous arrests of Christians took place. The Council was composed of wives, mothers, or other close relatives of these prisoners. In 1966 in response to a massive wave of new arrests, the Council of Prisoners' Relatives was expanded to include a number of wives and mothers of the newly arrested Christians.

and to make sure the needs of prisoners' families were met. They also determined to publish special bulletins that would inform local churches all over the country about the needs and prayer requests of prisoners and their families.

After returning home from Moscow, Babushka told us about that meeting. She mentioned that all the ladies were well aware of the danger involved in such a ministry. One of the goals they set for themselves was writing petitions to government officials in defense of those who were persecuted for their faith. Although they clearly realized that none of them had legal training, they decided to go ahead, relying only on God's help.

The Council of Prisoners' Relatives began gathering information and compiling files on Christian prisoners, including their names, the number of children in their families, home addresses, the specific articles of the criminal code used for their sentencing, the number of years they were sentenced to, and their prison addresses. It was not easy to gather all this information in a country as enormous as the Soviet Union, so Christians from many local churches helped.

After becoming a member of the Council, Babushka became actively involved in writing petitions to the government.* Before long the other members elected her to be the president of the Council of Prisoners' Relatives, and our home became a refuge for all who were persecuted. Our address was passed to Christians all over the country and often the doorbell would ring in the middle of the night. When we opened the door, there would be the mother or wife of a newly arrested Christian from a faraway city. Babushka would welcome her, invite her to stay overnight, and set the table for a late supper. But first Babushka would ask what had happened, then they would pray and weep together. The next morning Babushka would help write a petition to the government and give practical advice on what kind of food to take to prison, and how to behave during the prosecutor's questioning and during the trial.

---

*The Council of Prisoners' Relatives had appointed five of its members—Aleksandra Kozorezova, Nina Yakimenko, Lydia Vins, Elizaveta Khrapova, and Klavdiya Kozlova—to sign the petitions to the government.

Christians came to our house from all over Ukraine, Russia, Belorussia, even as far as Siberia. Those who came would stay for two or three days, often with up to ten people from different cities spending the night at our house. We bought several folding cots and mattresses, and when that was not enough, the guests used our beds while we slept on the floor.

On one occasion a mother with two children came to Babushka. That woman had just lost her parental rights. Babushka immediately contacted a Christian family in a village that had agreed to hide children for a period of time. She also helped the mother write petitions to government officials and to Christians all over the world. But most important for the grief-stricken mother was that in this critical moment in her life she found support and practical help through the ministry of the Council of Prisoners' Relatives.

Our home was constantly under surveillance. Sometimes a car with secret police was parked right in front of our gate, and we were followed when we left the house. Back at home, nothing significant could be discussed aloud for we had reason to suspect that the KGB had planted listening devices in our house. All important messages were written on a piece of paper, which was immediately destroyed. From a very early age the children in our family learned the strict discipline: to always remember what not to discuss out loud, or what to do when you are followed by a secret police agent. We had to memorize all the addresses of friends since any written addresses were confiscated during house searches, which led to searches at those homes too. It was not safe to keep a journal or to entrust any kind of information to a piece of paper, because every written word became a target for the police during searches. Personal letters and family pictures were also confiscated.*

Government officials told Babushka to cease her involvement with the Council. If she did not obey, they threatened, she would be arrested, but she remained active in her ministry. As the years went by

---

*Because of the possibility of confiscation, all important family mementos were divided and entrusted for safekeeping to different people whose homes were less likely to be searched. But sometimes even those people became fearful and burned irreplaceable parts of the family archives.

and Babushka grew older, it wore on her to travel to other cities for meetings of the Council of Prisoners' Relatives and always to be concerned about concealing its archives to avoid their confiscation. Once, after returning from one such trip to Moscow, she recounted to us how their meeting had been raided:

A Christian family let us meet in their apartment on the sixth floor. Over twenty Christian women had gathered; they came from Russia, the Urals, Belorussia, Moldavia, Siberia, and Central Asia.

It was ten o'clock at night, and our discussion was still going. On the living room table lay petitions and other information on persecution from different cities. Suddenly we heard the doorbell. Our hostess looked through the peephole, ran back into the room, and exclaimed, "It's the police!" This phrase always made us shudder and scramble to find some quick solution. Lisa Khrapova grabbed all the papers and ran into the bedroom. The doorbell kept ringing; the banging on the door was getting louder, so our hostess had to open the door. Over twenty policemen and KGB agents rushed into the living room.

The man in charge was the chief prosecutor of Moscow. He announced who he was and introduced two other men: the KGB official in charge of the religious department and the chief of police for that region of Moscow. The prosecutor and the chief of police took off their hats, but the KGB man did not even show this common courtesy! He sat down at the table, still wearing his hat, and barked an order, "Put all your passports on the table!"

We obeyed his order. Then the prosecutor gave his speech. In general, he was quite civil even though he threatened to sentence each of us to three years in prison. At the end he said, "Stop being involved in such activities! Why are you meeting here? Why did you come to Moscow? Go back home; I don't want any of you left in Moscow by tomorrow night!"

The police superintendent filled out a report. After recording all our names and personal information, he was about to return our passports to us. But suddenly the KGB official snatched up all the passports, shoved them into his briefcase, and announced, "You will all have to report to the police station at 9:00 A.M. tomorrow to pick up your passports!"

This encounter with the officials had stretched well into the night. Finally they left, and we had to decide what to do next. Should we all disperse and spend the night at other Christian homes? How could we save the documents which Lisa had hidden in the bedroom? Even though the police hadn't searched the apartment this time, there was no guarantee they would not return in the morning to do a search. We prayed, asking for the Lord's guidance and then decided to leave by twos and threes and set out in different directions to spend the rest of the night with friends. In the morning, we met again at a new location and finished our conference. Praise the Lord, everything ended well!

As the number of prisoners increased, the work of the Council of Prisoners' Relatives grew accordingly. Three young Christian ladies in their mid-twenties started assisting Babushka as secretaries. Our house became their home base. They traveled to visit prisoners' families all over the country to gather information on persecution. As they visited families with many children, Babushka asked them to keep their eyes open for specific needs: did the kids have warm clothes and shoes? did the family have enough firewood and potatoes for the coming winter? was the roof leaking, or were there any other urgent repairs that the house needed?

The Council of Prisoners' Relatives tried to help in each case where the need was acute.* At Christmas the prisoners' families were sent parcels containing candy, cookies, dried fruit, and nuts to cheer up the children spending Christmas time without their papa.

---

*Each family regularly received a monthly allowance for living expenses from the local church. The amount depended on the number of children in the family.

The Vins family
in 1956:
Natasha with
Mama, Papa, and
Babushka

Three generations:
Natasha with
Grandmother
Lydia and Great
Grandmother
Maria

Natasha with Mama

Babushka with Peter in her garden

Babushka with Natasha and Peter in
the summer of 1962 when church
meetings in the forest began

Babushka with Natasha

Our family in 1963 after Papa was jailed for fifteen days. It was customary for
prisoners to have their heads shaved.

Papa in his prison uniform

Jane in 1967

Natasha, Mama, Peter, Lisa, and Jane before traveling to the Ural Mountains in 1968 to see Papa in the prison camp

Our home on Soshenko Street in Kiev

Worship service in the forest outside Kiev with Pastor Kovalenko preaching

Natasha and her friend Inna
traveling to see Babushka in
the prison camp

Lisa with her violin

Our youth group in the forest outside Kiev

Our camping trip

Vera Shuportyak after
her release from prison
in November 1968

41

Natasha with Luba Kosachevich while working with the underground Bible printing ministry in 1978

Jane at a very important milestone in her life—her first day of school as a first grader

Masha, our Sunday school teacher

Our church orchestra on a friend's wedding day

The Council of Prisoners' Relatives at our house in Kiev in 1979
shortly before we left for America

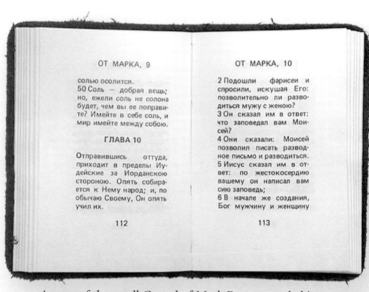

A copy of the small Gospel of Mark Papa smuggled into prison. Shown actual size, this book was easily hidden.

Alex with Papa during a meeting in the prison camp in 1976

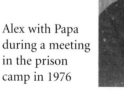

Georgi Vins on the first day of his release in New York City

Press conference in New York on April 28, 1979, the day after Georgi Vins' arrival in America

Jane

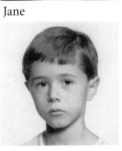

Alex

Peter with Alex,
cousin Irene, and
Eldar the dog
during our last days
at home in Kiev,
June 1979

Our first minutes of
meeting in America
as Papa thanks God
for our reunion,
June 14, 1979

Papa with Babushka and Alex on June 14, 1979,
the day our family arrived in America

Georgi Vins with President Ronald Reagan
in the White House in 1982

The Vins family in Elkhart, Indiana, in 1981

Mama and Papa in Chicago in
the summer of 1985

Alex and Peter at Jane's
wedding in 1988

Natasha Vins, March 2002

9

The summer of 1967 started with a great event—our Sunday school teachers announced that we were going on a three-day camping trip. The news brought such excitement! There were no Christian camps for kids in those days. The Young Pioneers' camps that our friends from school attended were not for us since Christian kids did not join the Pioneers. My friends and I were already teenagers and had never been to a summer camp. After we heard the news, we could not stop discussing how we would set up tents, roast potatoes over the fire, and swim in the river. And there would be a bonfire in the evenings!

Finally the long-awaited day arrived. Our teachers had chosen a place in the woods, by the small river Uzh, near Chernobyl. On the day of departure we met at the bus station. There were about sixty of us, ranging in age from ten to fifteen, accompanied by ten adults—our Sunday school teachers and some parents. A few of the grownups had left earlier in a car with tents and kitchen supplies. When we arrived at the campsite, the tents were already set up and delicious smells were coming from the dinner being cooked on the fire.

The place selected for the campsite was a clearing in the forest with the river flowing nearby. All of us were hungry after the long bus trip and just could not wait for dinner to be ready. I was assigned to a dishwashing team, and after the meal was over we collected all the spoons, bowls, and cooking pans and took them down to the river. There we scrubbed the dirty dishes with sand and rinsed them in the river.

Later everyone gathered by the bonfire and sang while Masha played her guitar. The summer night was quite still with the starry sky right above us. All this was so new and exciting to us city kids, who were used to the crowded streets and high-rise buildings of the big city.

When it was time to go to sleep, four people were assigned to a watch duty for the first half of the night. A second team would replace them until the morning. I was assigned to the second shift and now had to go to my tent, even though I longed to stay by the bonfire. How could anyone sleep on the first night of your very first camping trip? After tossing and turning for half an hour, Lena and I decided to crawl out of our tent and see what our friends on watch duty were doing.

The four of them were sitting by the fire, talking and reciting favorite poems. We were welcomed with an excited whisper, "Come and join us!"

Lena was not so sure. "But what if one of the grownups wakes up? We are going to be in big trouble!"

"Don't worry!" Alex calmed her down. "You and Natasha are doing the second shift anyway, so you just started a few hours earlier." We did not need much persuading, and Lena and I joined the rest of them by the fire.

Before we even noticed, our conversation drifted from poetry to a heart-to-heart talk about our dreams for the future and choosing our lives' paths. We were all close friends and shared mutual interests— our Bible studies, youth orchestra, evangelistic trips to remote villages. Being in our teens, we expected so much from life and were eager to peek into the future. "Let's meet like this, by a bonfire, in ten years." Vladimir suggested. "And then in twenty! Let's not lose each other, no matter what happens in our lives."

The time for the "changing of the guard" was quickly approaching, and the first four "watchmen" were supposed to go to bed. But no one wanted to sleep. We decided to wake up the rest of the second shift and all eight of us would stay by the fire till morning. Alex went to wake them up. When they came to the fire, Victor could not understand what was going on. He rubbed his eyes sleepily. "Why are there so many of us? Aren't some of you guys supposed to go back to your tents?"

"Don't you see?" Alex whispered. "It's safer when there are more of us! What if some drifters come to our camp?"

Victor burst out laughing, but we quieted him, "Hush! You are going to wake up the grownups, and they will send us all back to the tents!"

So we had a great time by the fire until sunrise. Some adults woke up around five o'clock and sent us all to bed. Nobody put up an argument, since by that time we could barely keep our eyes open. We immediately fell asleep, but two hours later it was time to get up. And thus began another happy day in our camping adventure. First we washed in the river and ate breakfast. After that came Bible lessons; then we learned some new Christian songs. We played games and swam in the river. After lunch Masha read to the teens a book about the first Christians in the catacombs, while the younger children listened to a story about Creation and drew pictures about it.

For dinner our cooks wanted to make a rice dish that required milk, but there was no milk. They also realized that the bread supply was low and decided to send several teens to the nearest village to buy bread and milk. Five of us volunteered to go. We took buckets for milk, bags to carry bread, and some money to pay for it all. But when we came back, our cooks were greatly disappointed. All the milk in our buckets had turned sour! In our ignorance we had combined milk bought from different people, not realizing that some cows were milked in the morning and some in the evening and that mixing it would spoil all the milk. However, we had brought fine fresh bread from the village, and that partially made up for our mistake of spoiling the milk.

After dinner we once again gathered around a bonfire. We sang, recited poems, and prayed together. To this day I treasure the memory of the close kinship that knitted us together. Suddenly one of the adults, Tanya's father, asked us to stop in the middle of a song. Everybody was troubled: what could have happened? He explained in a hushed voice that he had just been down by the river and seen two boats slowly floating past while their occupants shined flashlights on the banks as if they were looking for something. This alarmed him. Were they looking for us to report to the police that we had a Christian camp? He suggested that we should be cautious and go quietly to bed. The grownups decided to stay up all night.

We were awakened early in the morning. The news was disturbing. Several men had walked up to the fire in the middle of the night and asked questions about our camp. They said they were hunters who just got lost, but they did not carry any hunting gear with them. All this worried the adults and they decided to leave immediately after breakfast. We took down the tents, packed our backpacks, and by ten o'clock were on our way.

As we walked along the path through the woods toward the bus stop, several policemen appeared and blocked our way as they began questioning what we were doing there. The adults answered that we were returning home from a camping trip. The police announced that we were under arrest and led us to the road where a big truck with a canvas cover over its back was already waiting. Two police cars were there as well.

The police ordered us into the truck. Our leaders once again tried to explain that we had return bus tickets to Kiev, but it was useless to reason with the police. They were hurrying us, pushing us toward the truck. Even though we were crammed into it, not everyone could fit and some children were seated in the police cars. They drove us to a police station in Chernobyl, the closest town.

On the way to the police station, Natasha, the teacher of the younger kids, quickly passed to Luda and me the children's drawings of Creation. She asked us to tear them up and throw them away without being noticed. We understood the importance of this request. Our Sunday school teachers were responsible for the camping trip, and they could receive prison terms if any evidence was found that the camp was Christian in nature. These children's drawings could become strong evidence. Unfortunately, Luda and I did not get a chance to throw them away on the way to the police station, so we tucked them inside our jackets, hoping to do it later.

The police station turned out to be quite small, and we had to wait in the courtyard which was surrounded by a brick fence. A few people at a time were taken inside the building for interrogation. The rest of us plopped our backpacks on the ground and sat down on top of them.

Those who were taken for interrogation were ordered to bring their belongings with them. After finding out that people were being searched, Luda and I began to worry about what to do with the drawings. There was a restroom in the courtyard, and we decided this was our only chance of getting rid of the drawings. We tore them up and left them in the wastebasket, making sure that they looked inconspicuous.

The police searched us thoroughly; even the tents were taken out of their cases and examined. Each backpack was emptied out. Everyone, even the youngest children, was strip-searched. A policeman entered the women's restroom, found pieces of the children's drawings, and brought them into the interrogation room. The pieces were pasted together, and our leaders were told, "Here's evidence that you had a Christian camp!"

We were detained until dark, then taken to a bus stop and sent back to Kiev. We all arrived home after midnight. Thus ended the first-in-our-lives camping trip. But this wasn't the end of the story. The police opened a criminal case against Masha, whom they considered the person in charge of the camp, and she had to move to another city to escape arrest.

As teenagers, we struggled with conflicting feelings toward our persecutors. We grew up under complete lawlessness: in front of our eyes, policemen disrupted our church services, arrested Christian leaders whom we respected, and tried them as criminals. When we were young kids, it was simply terrifying to see men in police uniforms suddenly appear in the midst of a worship service, shouting, beating up Christians, and throwing them into the police cars. As the years passed and we became teenagers, our reaction to any kind of injustice intensified.

While waiting in the courtyard of that Chernobyl police station, we had tried to argue with our guards, asking them, "On what grounds is everything forbidden for children from Christian families? We are not even permitted to go camping! Why?" We defended our rights with such zeal that sometimes even harsh words slipped out during our interaction with the police.

This troubled our Sunday school teachers, and more than once they talked to us about having the right attitude toward our persecutors. They gave us assignments to search through the New Testament and to write reports on how Christ, the apostle Paul, and the New Testament church reacted to the enemies of the gospel. Our elderly pastor addressed this subject in a sermon, emphasizing how Christ, dying on the cross, prayed for His tormentors, "Father, forgive them; for they know not what they do." But for us it was still a constant struggle to have the right attitude toward the persecutors.

10

In October of 1967 Babushka and I traveled to the Ural Mountains to visit Papa at his prison camp. Our train pulled into Kizel late at night. We waited at the train station till morning to take the first bus as far as Talyi, the last town where all roads end and the taiga starts. Papa's prison camp was located twelve kilometers north of Talyi. The only way of getting to the camp was by a narrow-gauge railway. The "train" that occasionally traveled on it consisted of an engine followed by several open-air rail cars loaded with lumber.

Talyi was a small town with only a few streets, none of which were paved. It had been drizzling for several days, and the streets had been churned into mud. The houses along the streets were dark, water-soaked log huts with small, crooked windows. The people walking by also looked drastically different from the people I was used to seeing on the streets of Kiev. Both men and women in Talyi were dressed in black padded jackets and high rubber boots covered with mud. Their faces looked dismal and unfriendly. All this gloominess was so depressing.

How I longed to be back home! When Babushka and I left Kiev on a sunny autumn day, the chestnut trees were turning golden, and dahlias and chrysanthemums were blooming brightly in our garden. In the evening as we rode to the train station, the city center had been flooded with light from the large windows of the high-rise buildings and glowing streetlights. What a contrast it was to this forsaken place in the Urals. The only bright spot here was the anticipation of our visit with Papa.

When Babushka asked directions to the railroad, she was pointed to a wooden hut, which was "the station." Several people were already waiting there. In response to Babushka's question about the train schedule, they just laughed. Someone explained that there was no schedule, you simply had to wait till a train came. The wait could be for an hour or two, or for a whole day.

We waited for several hours. Our numerous pieces of luggage were spread around us. We had brought winter boots and warm clothes for Papa since winters in the Urals were severe, along with salami, lard, and canned food that could last him for a while in camp. Babushka had packed some bread, cheese, and fruit to feed Papa during our visit in case the guard would permit it. We also had some personal items to last us the whole week of traveling. That's how we ended up with so much luggage—a suitcase, a backpack and a large duffle bag.

When the train finally arrived, some men helped us load our luggage onto one of the open-air rail cars; then I climbed aboard. With the help of two men, Babushka climbed on too. The train ride through the taiga lasted for over an hour. With a cold wind blowing and rain pouring down on us, it was not long before everyone was thoroughly soaked and shivering in the cold.

Finally, in a clearing of the taiga we saw a tall barbed-wire fence that surrounded the camp, and a few small houses for the guards and their families. This was Anyusha, the tiny settlement around the prison camp.

Only Babushka and I were getting off at Anyusha. Our fellow passengers helped us to unload our luggage. The train left, and we stood all alone by the railroad tracks, looking for a place to hide from the rain. I noticed a small wooden hut close by. When we knocked, there was no answer. Babushka tried the door. It was not locked, so we entered, realizing that this was the waiting room for relatives who came to visit prisoners at the camp.

The hut consisted of one room with a wood-burning stove, a wooden table with a few benches by it, and a metal bed with a black, dirty mattress. To our surprise, a fire was burning inside the wood stove, and the room was warm and dry. I took off my wet coat and hung it by the stove. Babushka immediately went to hunt for the administration building to find out when we could see Papa. She came back an hour later very upset. The camp director had refused to give her permission for a visit, stating that Papa had broken the rules: during a search in the barracks the guards had found his notebook with a few Bible verses written in it.

Babushka pleaded with him not to deny us a visit after the three-day journey from Ukraine. But the camp director was extremely brusque and told her to get out of his office immediately and not waste his time. So, what were we to do now? Where should we turn for help? As we prayed and committed everything to God, Babushka decided to spend the night in this cabin and in the morning try to reason with the camp director again. We hoped that he would change his mind and allow us a visit with Papa.

It was growing dark when I looked out the window and saw rows of prisoners coming out of the taiga. Soldiers with rifles and large watchdogs guarded each work crew returning to camp after a day of logging. Babushka and I stepped outside our cabin, hoping to get at least a glimpse of Papa from a distance. But we could not recognize him amidst the crowd as all the prisoners were dressed in the same black padded jackets and caps, blending into a colorless mass. We stood on the porch for a long time until the last team of prisoners had disappeared behind the barbed-wire fence.

We settled for the night on the only bed in the room, using our sweaters as pillows and coats as blankets. The bed was so narrow that it was difficult even to move. In the middle of the night bedbugs started falling down from the ceiling, so we hardly slept at all. Early in the morning we once again stood on the porch, watching the prisoners file out of the camp row by row and disappear in the forest on their way to work. As on the previous evening, we did not recognize Papa among them.

At nine o'clock Babushka went to speak to the camp director. She returned very soon, telling me that this time he had been more civil but still would not permit a visit with Papa. He said that only the headquarters in Talyi could grant such permission. So we had to return to Talyi. But what to do with all of our luggage? Would we have to drag it with us? If we left it in the hut, it might be stolen by the time we returned. And would we even come back if the permit for a visit was not signed at headquarters?

On top of all our troubles, Babushka woke up that morning with a sharp pain in her lower back, probably from riding on an open platform in rain-soaked clothes in the cold wind. Now she could barely walk, and I would have to carry all the bags by myself. Finally Babushka decided to leave some of our luggage in the cabin, taking only the most valuable things. We repacked and left a full suitcase under the bed. I still had to carry a backpack and the large duffle bag.

We stood by the tracks waiting for more than an hour. Fortunately, the rain had stopped, and the sun was even peeking through the clouds. Two officers from the camp were also waiting for the train. Finally the officers decided that it was futile to wait there. The only alternative was to walk along the tracks to the next junction where the tracks going by the camp joined the main line. More trains traveled on that major line, and any one of them could give us a ride to Talyi. "It's about five kilometers from here to the junction," one of the officers informed us, as they took off walking along the tracks.

But for Babushka and me, it was not that simple to get going as it was for those strong forty-year-old men. First, I found a sturdy walking stick that Babushka could lean on. Then she helped me hoist the backpack onto my shoulders. The large duffle bag was still sitting on the ground. Babushka shook her head. "How are you going to carry all this for five kilometers? You are only fourteen. How in the world are we going to make it to the main line?" But what other choice did we have? We prayed and began plodding along the tracks.

We had been trudging for about an hour, stopping frequently to rest, when all of a sudden we heard a train whistle. We stepped aside and began waving frantically for the train to stop, but it was already slowing down. Because all the rail cars were loaded with logs, the engineer suggested that we climb into the engine compartment with him. Within an hour we reached Talyi, rejoicing that the Lord had so unexpectedly spared us from hours of walking.

In Talyi I stayed by the train tracks with the luggage, while Babushka, leaning on her stick, went searching for the prison camp's headquarters. The administrator there took pity on her and signed his permission for a visit. She came back to where I waited very excited, and we prayed that the next train would arrive soon.

It was growing dark by the time we reached the gates of Papa's camp. Since permission for a visit had been granted by the regional camp administrator, we were immediately led through the entrance. We were searched and taken into the room where visits took place. An officer entered the room, greeted us politely, and explained that he would be present during our visit. Then a guard led Papa in. He looked exhausted, but his eyes sparkled with happiness when he saw us.

The officer informed us that our meeting would last for two hours. He also warned that we were not allowed to discuss the conditions in the camp. Babushka asked for the officer's permission to let Papa eat some home-cooked food she had brought. Even though this was not usually allowed during a short visit, the officer told her to go ahead.

The following two hours flew by very quickly, as Papa wanted to find out all the family news and about his friends and the church. Unfortunately, there were many things we could not discuss in front of the officer, who did not leave us for even a minute.

Very abruptly came the officer's announcement that the visit was now over and it was time for us to leave. We prayed together and hugged Papa. As Papa returned to his barracks, Babushka and I made our way back to the hut. We spent another night there and the following morning began our long journey back to Ukraine.

11

Besides Papa and our pastor, Vasily Zhurilo, nine other believers from our church who were actively involved in the ministry were imprisoned in 1966. The youngest was Vera Shuportyak, one of the Sunday school teachers. At the time of her arrest, Vera was nineteen. The court sentenced her to two and a half years in prison camps. In November of 1968, after serving her term, Vera was finally released.

Vera's return home became a time of celebration for the whole church. At the first Sunday service she attended, Vera thanked everyone for prayers and the encouraging letters that she had received in prison camp. The youth group had organized a special reception for Vera, eager to hear her stories and ask questions. We felt like she was one of us. At the moment of arrest Vera had not been much older than we were now. We wanted to ask her about prison life and how she felt when the door of her cell was first locked behind her.

As the youth group got together, Vera started her story from the day of her arrest on May 17, 1966. That day police had imprisoned hundreds of Christians who had come to Moscow to request a meeting with high government officials.*

---

*In the 1960s the Soviet government intensified the persecution of Christians throughout the country, and it was suggested by church leaders that each local church send several members from its congregation to Moscow on May 16, 1966, to represent them before the government officials. After the delegation gathered on that day in front of the government headquarters, Christians requested a meeting with the head of the government. The delegation's goal was to give Mr. Leonid Brezhnev documents containing facts concerning persecution all over the country and to request that a governmental commission be formed to investigate the incidents of disrupted services, arrests, house searches, the confiscation of Bibles and religious literature, and other forms of persecution of Christians.

Vera told us how it all happened: "Several of us were traveling from Kiev. When our train arrived in Moscow, some Christians met us and gave directions to the Central Committee government building. In a matter of half an hour, more than four hundred Christians had gathered in front of it. Upon our request Mr. Stroganov, the front office supervisor, came out and announced that we would not be permitted to meet with Mr. Brezhnev. Our delegation was severely beaten by the KGB, and all of us were arrested.

"Before I left for Moscow, our pastors had asked me to take notes on everything that happened. From the start I began making brief notes in my notebook. At the police station the KGB officer who searched me found my notebook. Flipping through the pages he said, 'This is enough evidence to sentence you!' I was taken to prison.

"Five other Christian women, all members of our delegation, were in my cell. We prayed together and shared our impressions of recent events. My first interrogation took place on May 21. I was informed that a criminal case had been opened against me."

We were captivated by Vera's story. Victor could not wait any longer and asked, "Vera, what were you feeling during your first days in prison?"

Vera smiled and continued: "Many things made a tremendous impression during those first days in Lefortovo prison. I didn't know the prison rules, which turned out to be quite strict. I was especially afraid of the beatings. It was terrifying even to imagine it. The prison was old with massive walls and gloomy cells; everything was rather depressing. For three months before my trial I was mostly alone in my cell. Only occasionally did I have a cellmate for a day or two.

"Being an old prison, Lefortovo had an excellent library that had been there since the time of the czar. It contained many classical books by both Russian and foreign writers. The books were unabridged; most were published before the revolution and Soviet censorship. Some old books included quotations from the Bible, and those were invaluable since my Bible had been confiscated when I was arrested. I read a lot while awaiting trial and didn't feel lonely. I was only worried about my mom, knowing how anxious she must be about me.

"The trial took place in August. I was accused of actively participating in the Christian delegation as a correspondent. This was presented as breaking the law governing religious groups. As a result I was sentenced to two and a half years in prison camps.

"I look upon my whole prison experience as a valuable school of life. It's a totally different world. There you start to view things from a totally different perspective, such as the value of the human soul or what is really important in life. In prison you mature quickly. I was nineteen when I was arrested, and after only several weeks in prison I began to feel more experienced and able to understand life better."

Then Inna asked, "Vera, what was your most difficult experience in prison or in camp?"

Vera was silent for a while, then replied: "The most awful experience in prison life is the 'transit,' when prisoners are transported to a new location. I was shipped from Moscow to the Mordovski prison camp. Several dozen of us were crowded in a train car designed to transport prisoners. Ludmila from Orel, another member of our delegation, was traveling with me. She had the same sentence, and we were both going to the same camp.

"After we arrived at Potma, police cars transported us to the transit prison. The prison was old and filthy. Our cell was completely packed. The only empty bunks that Ludmila and I could find were beside the toilet. It was very late, so we prayed and lay down to sleep. Next to us was the bunk of an older woman with a hump on her back. She paced back and forth in our corner of the cell, telling her life story. This was her fourteenth imprisonment. She would get out of prison, steal something again, and end up back in prison.

"So here I was listening to her story and feeling a lump in my throat, trying to suppress tears. Probably I was just totally exhausted by the inhuman conditions around me. Finally, when I could not hold the tears back any longer, I began to sob. Ludmila also started crying. It took me a whole hour to calm down. That was like an emotional breakdown.

"The women around us became upset. 'Why do they put such young girls in these nasty cells? And for what? They believe in God;

just think what a *crime* it is! Calm down, girls! You will make it just fine in camp.'

"Quietly, Ludmila and I began to remind each other of verses from the Bible: 'Let not your heart be troubled: ye believe in God, believe also in me. In my Father's house are many mansions,' John 14:1–2. 'For I know the thoughts that I think toward you, saith the Lord, thoughts of peace, and not of evil, to give you an expected end,' Jeremiah 29:11."

By now Vera was bombarded with questions from all sides. But it was time to go home, since the youth meeting had already gone for too long. Vera agreed to answer one last question which came from Alex. "Vera, is it true that life in prison is just filled with difficulties? And every day there is only gray and bleak? Can't you remember anything bright?"

Vera smiled, "I indeed had some bright moments in the midst of the harsh reality of camp life. One event left a most vivid memory. On a cold winter night, after everyone in our barracks had already gone to sleep, guards came in and ordered us to get dressed and line up outside. It turned out that several train cars loaded with coal had arrived and had to be unloaded by morning. The women began to complain. Everyone was exhausted after a long workday and grumbled at the prospect of this unexpected night shift. But as prisoners we had no control over our lives and had to submit to orders.

"The assignment turned out to be quite strenuous. The temperature was extremely cold, and the chunks of coal had frozen together. We had to separate them with our bare hands. We worked for hours until all the coal was unloaded. It was close to daybreak when we were released to return to our barrack for a short rest before a new workday.

"My arms and back were stiff. As I climbed onto the top bunk, my only desire was to get under a blanket and close my eyes. My pillow was right by the window, and I looked outside. An old birch tree right by my window was illuminated by a streetlight. A small, frost-covered branch was reaching toward me. It scratched softly against my window. For me it was like God's smile. I felt afresh His presence and tender care, and was able to fall asleep peacefully until it was time to get up."

I did not ask Vera any questions during that meeting. I sat in a corner and just listened, comparing everything she was saying with what was going on in my heart. At the moment I was going through a challenging time of doubts about the validity of the Christian faith. Two years earlier a new mathematics teacher had come to our school. A recent graduate from the university and a devoted member of the Komsomol, the Communist Youth League, she was amazed to discover a "sectarian" in seventh grade. She determined to change my mind.

Her tactics for re-educating me were quite different from those used earlier. Shelya Abramovna never humiliated me in front of my classmates. On the contrary, she made every effort to win my confidence, to become a friend. She would strike up a conversation during recess hour or when classes were over.

After finding out that I loved to read, she began discussing with me the books of my favorite writers, Konstantin Paustovski, Alexander Green, or Antoine de Saint-Exupéry. In our discussions I was interested to know her opinion and to express my own. I was also pleasantly surprised at how tactful she was. She never brought up the subjects of religion or my faith in God as all my other teachers did when they talked to me.

Gradually Shelya Abramovna was becoming my confidante. I valued her opinions and began to look forward to our conversations during recess. Apparently she also sensed my growing trust and started to move into previously untouched areas. Once she asked for my opinion of Ethel Voynich's book *The Gadfly*. That was one of my favorite books at the time. I was impressed with the main character, Arthur, a young Italian revolutionary who was called Gadfly. I admired his courage and dedication to his ideas, and I felt pity for the Catholic priest Montanelli, especially at the climax of the book when he had to sign his approval for Arthur's death sentence. Shelya Abramovna severely condemned the priest and for the first time openly spoke about the harmful effects of religion.

As a result, I started to avoid her. But Shelya Abramovna insisted that our conversations continue. She cited many arguments that the Bible was outdated and full of scientific mistakes. "You have to understand, Natasha," she tried to convince me, "that Christianity is the

fate of feeble and spineless individuals! Only those who lack a sense of personal value and are unable to confront the challenges of life turn to religion. They just want to dump their problems on God. For them God is like a crutch for a crippled invalid!"

She also used another type of argument, "Just think—what kind of future awaits you if you don't turn away from religion? Will you be able to get higher education? I doubt it. It was a serious mistake that your parents were allowed to graduate from Soviet universities with their religious beliefs. But today this would not happen! Do you realize that you are denying yourself the possibility of an interesting, creative profession? Why should you ruin your life?"

I thought a lot about what she said and was going through inner turmoil. Even though in my heart I agreed with my teacher's arguments, during our discussions I would always defend Christians. Papa was very dear to me, having been deprived of freedom for his faith. Fresh in my memory were the gloating exclamations of KGB agents when they would find a Bible during a house search, or the cruelty of the policemen who disrupted our worship services. I realized that to openly agree with my teacher in her verbal assaults on Christians would mean to side with the persecutors. I could not do that.

But on the other hand, there seemed to be valid reasons that kept me from choosing the Christian path. I loved my literature classes. We had a wonderful teacher who taught us to appreciate good books, to analyze the strong points of classical writers, to think creatively. She assigned us thought-provoking essay topics for her class, and I enjoyed working on those assignments.

Tanya Savenkova, my best friend at school, was also interested in literature. She planned to go to university and specialize in translating English novels.* Tanya was always talking about the interesting opportunities such a profession would give her. All this greatly attracted me. But I knew that if I made a Christian commitment all the doors for pursuing a university education would be closed for me.

---

*The schools had a special emphasis on learning English as a second language, starting in first grade.

My parents, being Christians, were able to receive higher education because they entered university soon after the Second World War, when the state needed educated people to replace the millions who were killed at the front. Now times had changed. For my generation the situation was quite different. I knew of many instances in which Christians, after being admitted into the university, were kicked out as soon as they refused to join the Komsomol. Thinking all this over, I came to the conclusion that I was not ready to part with my dreams for the future. Making such a sacrifice for God's sake seemed too high a price.

12

I was already sixteen in May of 1969 when Papa was scheduled to be released. In a letter to Papa Babushka described our home life that spring:

> The children eagerly await your return. As always, Jane misses you more than anyone else. She is four now and has grown so much. What a charming and unpretentious child she is! Her eyes are sparkly, and she is quite a talker. She just bubbles with happiness. Yesterday she said, 'What, Papa isn't home yet? Just wait, he'll be here in five minutes! Everybody watch the clock.' Some mornings she will announce that she saw you in her dreams. But mostly she likes to tell how she wrestled you down during our recent visit. Everyone is already asleep as I'm writing you. May God strengthen you and give you courage. All our friends send you greetings.

Several days before Papa's release, Mama set off on the long journey to his prison camp. She was taking money for his ticket and a change of clothes so that he would not have to travel across the country in his prison uniform. Mama arrived a day early and was able to pass a note to Papa through a prisoner on work release. She wrote that she would meet him by the camp's entrance at nine o'clock the next morning as she had just been instructed at the administration office. She also let Papa know of her plans to stay overnight in a hut for prisoners' families by the railroad.

As Papa read in her note that the hour of his release had been set by camp officials, his suspicions that the warden wanted to search him personally were confirmed. During his three years of imprisonment Papa had accumulated a bundle of papers that were important to him, including personal letters and a few notebooks with his new

poems. He wanted to bring these notes home but knew all too well that on the day of release he would be searched, and all his papers could be confiscated. He prayed for God's protection of his prison archives.

Suddenly he had an idea. Technically, his prison term would end at midnight and at the first minutes of a new day he was a free man. So he decided to pack his belongings in advance and go to the main gate a few minutes after midnight. He could not sleep at all that night, and near midnight he approached the gate with his heart pounding. Would his plan work?

At the main gate Papa told the guard that he wanted to see the officer on duty. It turned out that the officer that night was one who had been friendly to him. The officer was interested in the Bible, and they had had several discussions about the existence of God.

"Citizen commander," Papa said. "My prison term ended five minutes ago and I would like to leave the camp right away!"

"Very well, Vins," the officer good-naturedly replied. "Let me check your records."

He pulled a file off the shelf, checked it and smiled.

"Yes, that's right. Congratulations, you are free!"

He shook Papa's hand. Then he signed and handed him the release documents.

As the gates were opened and Papa stepped into the night, for the first few minutes he just walked. He didn't know where he was going, and only wanted to get as far away from the camp as he could. He held his bag with its precious papers close to his heart, thanking God for this deliverance. As his eyes adjusted to the darkness, he started walking toward the railroad to look for the hut where Mama was staying that night. When he knocked on the door, Mama was alarmed but then recognized him and opened the door. Papa told her how he had managed to get released before the morning. They prayed together and began packing to leave on the first train.

A few days later they arrived home. Everybody was excited to see Papa. At the next worship service in the woods he was asked to

preach. After the service was over, people pulled out sandwiches, homemade pies, apples, tea in thermoses, and everyone ate lunch together. Papa was asked to tell about his prison experiences, and the time of fellowship lasted until evening.

Our home life took a new turn after Papa's release. Left behind was the constant worry for Papa, our rare visits in prison camps, and waiting for his letters. Lisa and Jane livened up; Papa played with them and told them stories. The most exciting event was a daylong excursion to the zoo. Peter and I interacted with Papa on a different level. Years earlier, when Papa had to leave Kiev, I was ten and Peter was seven. Now that Papa was back home six years later, he longed to reestablish a close, trusting relationship with his grown children. It was important for him to understand our new interests and activities.

One evening Papa asked me, "In a year you will graduate from high school. What's next? Are you thinking of going to college? You always liked the medical profession. How about studying nursing?"

"I am not sure. Of course, I like nursing. But on the other hand, I studied English for ten years, and I wish to put it to use. I would like to translate books. There is just such a department at the Institute of Cultural Development."

"But I am sure you know that as a Christian you will not be allowed to get a job in that field."

"Papa, I've been wanting to talk to you about this since you came back, but I could never bring myself to mention it. I didn't want to upset your first days at home."

"What do you mean, Natasha? Let's talk openly. I am your father; I love you, and it's important for me to know what's going on in your heart."

"I don't want to shock you, but the Christian commitment is your way of life, Mama's, Babushka's, but so far it's not mine. I'm not sure it will ever be. I have doubts about the validity of Christianity. And not just that. I keep wondering, is it worth losing the opportunity for a good education? What chance would I as a Christian have for an interesting, creative profession? None!"

"Of course, your education and future profession are important," Papa answered. "But that's not as crucial as your relationship with God. What has led you to all these doubts, Daughter?"

"There is a teacher at our school whom I respect a lot. She challenged me to rethink what I have accepted without question from being brought up in a Christian home. For example, I couldn't disprove Shelya Abramovna's arguments that the Bible is outdated and contains many scientific mistakes. She also thinks that Christianity is the fate of weaklings who cannot overcome the blows of life and need God as a crutch."

I stopped, realizing that I had said too much. I was afraid that my doubts would disturb Papa. That's why I had not shared them at home before. But his reaction was very calm. "Fine, let's talk about whether it's true or not. Many Christians, whom you've known all your life, have the courage to take a stand for their beliefs. They go against the current in our atheistic society and surely pay the price. Can you call them weaklings?"

I could not refute this. But all the same, I still had more pertinent questions. Papa was ready to listen.

"You are right; I can't call most Christians weaklings. But tell me, why do you believe in God? Only because Babushka raised you to believe it? Did you automatically accept the faith of your parents? Why is Christ so important to you? Why do Christians think that they have all the answers? What right do they have to think that they are smarter than everyone else? Smarter than even scientists or writers?"

"Natasha, I'm deeply convinced that God exists. The universe has a Creator. There are numerous scientific supports for it. But let's discuss that some other time, and now let me try to explain why the person of Jesus Christ is so precious to me.

"During the crisis moments of imprisonment, when I was looking death in the eyes, I realized anew what a dear price Christ paid for our salvation. Often after long, exhausting days of chopping down trees in the forest, the guards would lead us five to seven kilometers back to camp through deep snow. At times I didn't even have the strength to take another step. On top of exhaustion, I had a hernia, so walking was extremely painful. There was just a desperate cry in my heart, 'Lord, help me! Give strength not to collapse!' In moments like that I imagined how Jesus felt, falling down under the weight of His cross. With new freshness it became apparent to me how much our salvation cost Him. Do you see, Daughter, why Jesus is more precious to me than life?

"There is another thing that's hard to handle in prison. You are surrounded by people twenty-four hours a day. Just imagine day after day, month after month. It's impossible to be left alone even for a moment. The barracks are packed with dozens of prisoners who are constantly smoking, arguing, playing cards, cursing. At times I desperately wanted to get away from all of that, to be alone, especially when my heart was heavy or I felt sick.

"In those moments I used to think that even wounded animals crawl deep into the woods to hide, especially when they are dying. Man is even more desperate in his need for privacy. Hurt by the lack of it in prison, I better understood the depth of Christ's suffering on the cross, exposed to the hostile crowd. Death is always tormenting; a person in agony needs comfort and care of loved ones. Even more essential is the absence of curious harsh stares of strangers, so that the dying person is not forced to suppress moans of pain.

"But in His dying hours Christ became the laughingstock of strangers hungrily watching for expressions of pain on His face. How their sarcastic shouts hurt Him: 'If you are the Son of God, come down from the cross! You saved others, why can't you save yourself?' It's hard to imagine how Christ, in such deathly torment, was still able to cry out of pity for this mob, 'Father, forgive them; for they know not what they do.' This Jesus I love, Natasha. This is the Lord I serve."

I thought a lot about Papa's words. We often talked about things that troubled me. Papa always had time for me. By the spring of 1970, a year had passed since his return from prison. I was finishing my last year in school and was looking forward to graduation. The crucial time of doubts continued. I was still searching. My parents' Christian path could not automatically become mine. I had to find my own answers to all these troubling questions.

In recent years a tradition had been established in Kharkov to hold big youth rallies during May Day holidays. That spring about thirty people from our youth group were planning to go. Papa suggested, "Why don't you go as well?" I agreed, but was mostly interested in the overnight train ride with friends, having fun and talking until sunrise.

Kharkov welcomed us with a bright, sunny morning. At the train station we got directions where to go next and took a commuter train. After getting off, we walked through the woods until we reached a large meadow where a lot of young people had already gathered. As the service began, a youth choir sang and a brass band played. It sounded like a joyful celebration.

One preacher's message grabbed my attention: "Who is Jesus Christ to you?" He was saying, "Perhaps, for you, Jesus is only a great teacher of moral principles. Or do you consider Him the most outstanding person who ever lived on the earth? But it's not just that. Jesus left the glory of heaven and came to our planet for a much greater reason. He died on the cross to become a personal Savior for each of us. He wants to remove your burden of sin and to become your best Friend today!"

An intense battle raged in my heart. I understood that the Lord was speaking directly to me. He wanted to take my sins away and receive me into His family. I remembered what Papa had said about the price Jesus had to pay for our salvation. Everything inside me was reaching out to God. My former doubts about the validity of Christianity seemed so puny and meaningless. I began praying silently, "Lord, please forgive me and take away this burden of sin. Come into my life. I want to belong to You!"

Tears streamed down my face as the joy of belonging to Jesus filled my heart. Only then did I notice that the preacher was inviting people to come forward to pray for forgiveness of sin. Many teenagers responded. I, too, went forward and got down on my knees to thank God that now I was His child. After I prayed, I opened my eyes and saw my childhood friends next to me. They likewise had given their hearts to Christ that day.

When the service in the forest came to an end, it was time to catch our train for Kiev. All our seats were in the same train car, and until late that night we shared our impressions of the day. The train arrived in Kiev early in the morning. The subway was not open yet, but the first buses were already running. I just could not wait to get home and tell Papa, Mama, and Babushka that now I finally had peace with God because Jesus had become my Savior.

It was still very early when I rang our doorbell. Papa opened the door right away. I gave him a big hug. "Papa, I'm a Christian now!"

There were tears in his eyes as he said, "Natasha, how I've been praying for you these days!" We walked into the living room, got down on our knees, and thanked God for His wonderful gift of salvation.

13

At the end of August in 1970, a policeman knocked at our door. He handed Papa a notice to appear the next day at the prosecutor's office for questioning. That evening Papa met with the ministers from our church. They discussed the situation and all agreed that he should leave Kiev and continue his ministry among the persecuted churches "underground." Papa spent the night at a friend's house and left Kiev early the next morning.

Once again we had to adjust to life without Papa.

That fall Peter started the eighth grade, Lisa the third. Little Jane had turned five. After my graduation in May I got a job as an apprentice in the drafting department of a design firm. Mama worked at home weaving tote bags that were sold at the market. Babushka was actively involved in the ministry of the Council of Prisoners' Relatives.

On November 27th I turned eighteen. My friends from the youth group came, and we celebrated together. Life was exciting and moving full speed ahead with our orchestra practices, Bible studies, and evangelistic trips to small churches in remote villages.

The morning of December 1 began as usual. I left for work, Peter and Lisa went to school, and Babushka stayed home with little Jane. Mama had left a couple of days earlier for a brief visit with Papa and was still gone. That afternoon the first snow started to fall. At the end of the workday I joined the stream of hundreds of my co-workers flowing out of the high-rise building of our design firm. As I walked to the bus stop, I enjoyed the beauty of the first snow. It was exciting to watch the kids sledding and the older boys having snowball fights. Winter was finally here!

Each Tuesday our youth group met for Bible studies. So that evening I went straight from work to Lilia's apartment, where we were supposed to meet. There were about twenty of us. The topic turned out to be so engaging that we lost track of time, and our Bible study ended later than usual.

As we left the apartment a few people at a time, so as not to attract the attention of neighbors, Lena and I traveled in the same direction. Our bus ride took almost an hour, and we had enough time for a good chat. Lena got off two stops before me. I traveled to the end of the line. It took me about ten minutes to walk from the bus stop to our house. I walked fast. Babushka always worried when I returned home late. And today, because of the first snow, traffic was slower than usual, and it was almost eleven o'clock.

We lived on the outskirts of the city, and as usual at such a late hour, our street was empty. From a distance I noticed two police cars parked next to our gate. "Here it comes! Another house search!" I thought anxiously and started walking even faster. A policeman was standing by our gate. He tried to stop me. "Where are you going? Show your documents!"

"I'm going home. I live here," I answered, walking right past him.

The door of our house was wide open in spite of the cold, snowy evening. Another policeman was stationed by the door and once again I heard, "Stop! Where are you going?" My worries intensified. Such unusual precautions from the police did not look like an ordinary house search. I walked through the hallway to the living room. Several KGB agents and two or three policemen stood there. The rumble of voices was in the air.

Finally, I saw Babushka. For some reason she was standing in the middle of the room with her winter coat on. Babushka rushed to me.

"I'm so glad you are finally home! I was worried they would take me away before you came back!"

"They are going to take you away? What are you talking about?"

"Natasha, I am under arrest! And Mama is not back yet. Look at the kids!" She pointed to the couch where little Jane was lying down, sobbing loudly. Next to her sat Lisa, who was also crying. Peter was standing by the table.

A KGB man, apparently the one in charge, as he was giving orders to others, began to rush Babushka. "Hurry up! That's enough good-byes! Time to go!" All of a sudden I realized that Babushka who was always a source of strength and courage to me, seemed drained of energy and perplexed. Suddenly I knew that all the responsibility now rested on me.

"Where are you taking her?" I turned to the man in charge. "She has a heart disease! She may have a heart attack in the police car. I'm going to go with her to see where you are taking her."

He talked it over with two other men and answered sternly. "Fine, you may come with her. But no one is going to drive you back home from the other end of the city. You will have to come home by yourself after midnight. That's it. Let's go!"

"I want to pray with the children before I leave," Babushka said.

"What? You want to pray?" The KGB officer snapped. "That's all we need right now."

I could not hold back any longer. "How dare you speak to her that way? Babushka is still in charge in her own home!"

Babushka and I held hands. Peter, Lisa, and Jane quickly joined us. I began praying out loud, asking the Lord to protect Babushka in all the dangers that lay ahead for her. This irritated the officials, but nobody interrupted us. Babushka also prayed and then hugged each of the children. As she walked out to the police car, she leaned on my arm. To our surprise, we saw an ambulance parked behind the police cars. It seemed that the KGB wanted to be prepared in case she had a heart attack.

As we walked up to the police car, I helped Babushka up the steps. When I, too, started climbing into the car, she suddenly looked back at the children and stopped me. "No, Natasha, you are not going with me. Just look at them." I turned around. Peter, Lisa, and Jane were standing in the snow with no coats or boots, just in thin sweaters and house slippers. Peter was holding his dog.

"You have to stay with them!" insisted Babushka. I did not object. I hugged her for the last time and joined the children. With a loud roar the police cars pulled away. We stood on the snow-covered street and watched them disappear into the distance. Then we slowly walked back into the empty house.

Later Babushka told us her first prison impressions. "We reached the prison after midnight. The police had to formalize my arrest: they took my fingerprints, mug shots, and completed the paperwork. That was a long procedure. At last I was led to a cell. With a large key the guard opened a metal door. I went in and looked around. The cell was barren and cold. Murky light was coming from a small light bulb on the ceiling. Two metal beds along the walls were without mattresses or pillows. I prayed and went to sleep just as I was, without taking off my coat or shoes.

"The next morning, the guard took me to my first interrogation. As I saw my interrogator enter the room neatly dressed and looking fresh after a good night's rest, I imagined what I must have looked like in my wrinkled coat after a sleepless night. That's how my prison journey began."

14

For three months before the trial Babushka was kept in Lukyanovskaya Prison. We received no word from her. Prosecutor Bekh was handling her case. The trial took place in March of 1971. As usual, the family was not notified concerning the day and location of the trial. Mama managed to find out about it after the trial had already begun. She called me at work, so I took the rest of the day off and hurried to the courthouse.

Later Babushka told us how she had been looking forward to seeing us as she was driven to the courthouse in a police car. And what a disappointment it was to be led by guards into the courtroom and not see even one familiar face. All the seats were filled with strangers who glared at her with hostility. When the hearing started, she asked the court to notify her family. But her request was ignored.

Babushka was accused for her involvement in the Council of Prisoners' Relatives and particularly for signing petitions to the government concerning the evidence of persecution. At the beginning of the trial she let the court know that, as the president of the Council of Prisoners' Relatives, she assumed full responsibility for all the documents that the Council had issued. In light of this she asked the court not to prosecute any other member of the Council, since most of them were mothers with large families.

Babushka was tried under Articles 138 and 187 of the Criminal Code of the Ukranian SSR. The accusations were based on four specific facts taken from petitions to the government. The prosecutor claimed that all these facts were fabricated, and consequently all the petitions by the Council of Prisoners' Relatives constituted slander of the Soviet State.

Babushka suggested that the court call as witnesses those who were victims in the cases described in the petitions. But the judge answered that there was no need to do that, since the court had already selected enough witnesses. Their choice was based upon the recommendations of the prosecutor.

The judge began questioning witnesses. There was not one Christian among them.

The witnesses were representatives of the prison camp administration when the petition described how a specific prisoner was beaten, denied visits with his family, and otherwise oppressed while in the prison camp.

The witnesses were policemen who participated in disrupting the worship services when the petition focused on the injuries Christians received as a result of brutally disrupted services.

The witnesses were representatives from the city administration when a petition mentioned the enormous fines levied upon retired Christians.

Of course, such witnesses emphatically denied their own inhumane actions. As a result the court came to the conclusion that since none of the witnesses confirmed the facts described by the Council of Prisoners' Relatives, these petitions to the government were indeed slanderous. Consequently, by signing such petitions, Lydia Vins was guilty of slander against the Soviet State.

Babushka tried to bring to the court's attention the absurdity of their choice of witnesses. Instead of calling to testify at least some individuals who had suffered the injustice, the court called in the offenders—precisely those whose brutal conduct was described in the petitions to the government. No wonder such individuals would deny all the facts.

Prosecutor Dolinsky interrupted her, "Vins, you are forgetting your place! You are the accused! It's not for you to give orders to the court whom to invite as witnesses."

The judge agreed with the prosecutor. "Vins, you will have a chance to testify at the end of the trial. That's when you can express your disagreements with the court. Not now!"

Babushka did not have a defense lawyer to represent her interests. Since all lawyers in the Soviet Union were atheists, in most cases they would collaborate with the prosecution rather than defend a Christian. At the beginning of her trial, Babushka told the court that she would assume responsibility for her own defense. The judge agreed to it, but during all three days of her trial, every time she tried to make a statement, she was rudely interrupted.

On the second day, when we arrived at the courthouse, we saw that several dozen Christians were already waiting outside. But only a few of them managed to get into the courtroom since it was filled with KGB agents who were admitted by showing special entry passes. Besides Mama and myself, only about ten other Christians were present at the trial.

Among them were two prisoners' wives—Zinaida Vilchinskaya and Seraphima Yudintseva, Babushka's co-workers at the Council of Prisoners' Relatives. When they learned that the trial had started, they took overnight trains to get to Kiev from Brest and Gorky.

On the last day Prosecutor Dolinsky delivered his closing allegations. His remarks were harsh and merciless. He insisted that Lydia Vins* had to be sentenced to five years of imprisonment. When Babushka was allowed to make her final statement, she said that for her any sentence would be a death sentence. Because of her heart condition, she explained, she would probably not survive even the first year of imprisonment. But she added at once that in no way did she regret the choice she had made to speak up on behalf of persecuted Christians.

The court sentenced Babushka to three years of imprisonment. Zinaida Vilchinskaya described later her impressions of the trial: "Lydia Mikhailovna conducted herself with such dignity that it was

---

*The name "Vins" is her last name and is the name used in the formal courtroom setting. In the following paragraph her friend refers to her more personally with the name "Mikhailovna" which literally means "the daughter of Mikhail."

hard to realize she was the accused. She answered the judge and the prosecutor with much wisdom and tact. In all, she did not just advocate herself, but rather all the persecuted Christians in our country.

"After the judge pronounced her sentence, several of us tossed flowers to her: carnations, snowdrops, and violets. Someone exclaimed, 'This is for your courage!' The bouquet of violets fell apart in the air, and the flowers landed gracefully on Lydia Mikhailovna's shoulders.

"I was sitting very close to the bench for the accused and decided to step right up to her and give her my bouquet. As I did it, I only managed to say, 'You were brave and steadfast during the trial!' And the guard shoved me away.

"We were ushered out of the courtroom while Lydia Mikhailovna remained there under guard. Many Christian friends were waiting outside. We joined them and from a distance saw a police car drive up to the entrance. A few minutes later she was led out of the building. She was holding the flowers.

"The young people began to sing a hymn. Lydia Mikhailovna waved at us. Then I noticed that she was trying to climb into the police vehicle, but was not able to as the steps were quite high. I realized that after months of imprisonment and all the stress of the trial she was too frail.

"Just then the guards that stood nearby helped her into the car, and she was gone."

After the trial Babushka was sent to a prison camp in Kharkov. As soon as we received a letter with her new address, I took two vacation days and went to Kharkov to see her and take a package with food and clothes. My friend Inna volunteered to go with me, and I was greatly relieved since I knew it would be a challenge to find the place. On top of that, I would be traveling with several heavy bags with food, medicine, and clothes for Babushka.

As we had anticipated, finding the prison camp was not simple. The address on the envelope was a post office box without a street address. The information booth at the train station could not tell us the location of such an institution. Finally we decided to pay a visit to a Christian family whose address I had brought along. We took a subway and then a bus, all the while carrying those heavy bags. How thankful I was that Inna was there to help.

Finally, with the assistance of local Christians we reached the camp. It was located on the outskirts of the city, not far from the airport. At once Inna and I got permission for a visit with Babushka. She walked into the room looking pale and exhausted, wearing a plaid prison uniform. But how excited she was to see us! Right away she started asking about everything that had happened at home since her arrest.

Babushka admitted that she was not feeling well and often had chest pains, especially at night. I asked her if she had to work. Babushka explained that everybody had to work in the camp. If she did not work, she would be transferred to a camp for invalids in a different town, and that place was infamous for its awful conditions. She was determined to work as long as she had strength in order to remain at the Kharkov camp. I told her I had brought some heart medication, and she asked me to leave it with the camp doctor.

The two hours of our visit flew by rapidly. When we parted, Inna and I were left with the impression that the following three years in prison camp would be difficult for Babushka to survive. After returning to Kiev, we reported to our church family about the visit. The church ministers decided to write an appeal to the government, asking for Babushka's release based on her poor health. They also emphasized in the petition that she had been sentenced unlawfully. More than two hundred believers signed the petition.

In June of 1971 thirty young people from our youth group were going to be baptized in a small lake in the middle of the forest on the outskirts of Kiev. I was one of them.

I woke up early that Sunday morning and looked out my window. The sun was already up. It was raining a little. But thankfully there were no heavy clouds, so I knew the weather would improve. I took the earliest bus to get to the lake. My friends had agreed to meet there an hour before the service to spend time in prayer on such a memorable day for us.

Almost all thirty of us were able to arrive early. After meeting at the bus stop, we walked through the forest toward the lake. By then the rain had stopped, and the leafy branches seemed to beckon to us as we walked. The lake sparkled in the sunshine. As we knelt under the trees by the water, each one prayed. Then we began sharing our favorite Bible verses with short testimonies of how that particular verse became special. Everyone felt that this time of fellowship before our baptism would remain in our memories forever.

Before long, other Christians began to arrive. Many carried flowers to present to us after the ceremony. Two tents were pitched for us to change in. By the time we came out and walked down to the lake, the whole congregation and many guests were there, over four hundred people. Our pastor read from the Bible about the significance of baptism, he prayed, and one by one we went into the water.

The pastor's voice triumphantly resounded across the lake, "Do you believe that Jesus Christ is the Son of God?"

"Yes, I believe!"

"On the basis of your faith I baptize you in the name of the Father, and the Son, and the Holy Ghost. Amen."

All this time the choir on the shore was singing quietly. A light rain had resumed again. When I stepped out of the water, an elderly lady whispered to me, "This rain represents showers of blessing!" After we changed inside the tents, the worship service began. For the first time in our lives we participated in communion. At the end of the service each of us was presented with flowers. That was a happy day! The only sad thought that crossed my mind was that neither Papa nor Babushka could share with me the joy of this day.

After I was baptized, I earnestly prayed for the Lord to show me how I could serve Him. Even though all my interests, as well as everyone else's in our youth group, were closely tied to the life of the church, I understood that God had a special task just for me. I talked about it with my pastor, and several weeks later was assigned to help a Sunday school teacher with one of the children's classes.

By the end of that summer of 1971, the question of my further education was also settled. Papa suggested that I apply to a nursing school. Taking into account that such training was on the level of junior college and was not considered equal to a university degree, we hoped that the KGB would not interfere and I would be able to finish. I passed the entrance exams and began classes in September. Luba, my friend from church, was also admitted, and we ended up in the same class. I enjoyed the lectures and especially the practical training at the hospital.

December 10, 1971, brought a happy addition to our family. My youngest brother Alex was born. We wrote Babushka about this event. She was very excited and began praying for God's special blessings upon the life of her newest grandchild.

15

In November of 1971 Babushka was transferred to a different prison camp in Dneprodzerzhinsk, where several barracks were designated for the elderly and invalids. This was the infamous camp she had heard so many negative reports about. As soon as I received this news, I decided to go see her the following weekend. Once again Inna volunteered to travel with me.

The camp was located on the outskirts of the town. As soon as Inna and I got there, we understood at once why Babushka was so afraid to end up in this particular camp. On one side of it was the city dump. On the other side stood a huge chemical plant with ten chimneys reaching high into the sky. Each chimney emitted billows of smoke—some gray in color, and others dirty yellow or reddish. Babushka later told us that when the wind was blowing from the direction of the chemical plant on hot summer days, one could hardly breathe.

The conditions here were much worse than in Kharkov's camp. The outhouses were located in a remote part of the camp yard. Doing personal laundry was difficult, and there was no place to dry it. Food was scarce and of poor quality. Babushka suffered from heart disease, but the medical station did not have the medications she needed. On my first visit I brought her heart medicine, and as in Kharkov's camp, I wanted to leave it with the doctor. To my surprise, this woman doctor treated me rudely. She refused to accept the medications and give them to Babushka when she needed them.

Also, Babushka had a recurring bladder infection. As a result she had to use the toilet several times during the night. This presented a real hardship, especially in the winter, as she had to get dressed, go outside, and walk to the outhouse across the camp yard. The wooden outhouses had many cracks in the walls through which the cold wind would blow. Most nights turned out to be sleepless and troublesome for Babushka. And during the day, even though she did not have to work, prisoners were not allowed to lie down on their beds. She had to sit in the barracks all day long and then would come another sleepless night.

There were other complications in the new camp that had not existed in Kharkov. One day we received a note from Babushka:

> My dear ones.
>
> With great sorrow I have to let you know that yesterday, on December 28, I was notified by a camp official—and they asked me to write you about it—that if my letters to you or your letters to me contain words like "God", "Jesus Christ," or phrases like "May God protect you," "May God bless you," "Wishing you a Merry Christmas," or any other religious phrases, then your letters won't reach me, and my letters won't reach you either. Based on that, they refused to let me read Lisa's Christmas card and letter that she sent me.
>
> That's all for now.
>
> With much love,
>
> your Babushka
>
> Dec. 29, 1971*

But the Lord had prepared a wonderful surprise for Babushka. On her very first day in the new camp, when her group of prisoners arrived, they were led to a quarantine barracks where the guards searched them. By the time the search was over, it was already past dinnertime and late. Some cold, leftover soup was brought from the prison kitchen. As the newcomers ate their soup, a local prisoner in her mid-thirties walked in, went straight to Babushka, hugged her and said, "Hello, Lydia Mikhailovna. My name is Vera. I am a Christian too and I was arrested for teaching Bible lessons to children. I heard you speak several years ago at the ladies' seminar in Kharkov."

---

*This was the only prison letter from Babushka that survived. All the other letters were confiscated during a house search soon after her release. That search was unexpected, and there was no chance to hide the letters. The text of this letter survived only because the Council of Prisoners' Relatives printed it in their information bulletin shortly after the letter was received.

They became inseparable. Vera treated Babushka as a daughter would. She helped her in any way possible and took care of her when Babushka was sick. Together they would find a quiet place to pray and encourage each other with the Bible verses they knew by heart.

But before long the camp administration started to prevent their meetings. Vera was even threatened with solitary confinement if she continued to visit the barracks for the elderly. But Babushka found a solution. Early in the morning, when the rows of prisoners were marched to work, she would step outside of her barracks and walk up and down the sidewalk. When Vera's work crew walked by, she would quickly whisper a Bible verse to Vera or say an encouraging word. Vera would smile at her, and that's how they carried on their secret communication.

I tried not to miss any scheduled visits with Babushka and traveled with the younger children to see her. Babushka's health was quite fragile. She could barely walk and had lost hope of surviving her imprisonment. She felt especially helpless after Vera was released. Without Vera's help and moral support, her last months of imprisonment became most difficult.

Babushka was permitted four family visits per year: two "personal visits" every six months when we could spend two days with her in a special barracks inside the camp, and two "general visits" that lasted two or three hours each. Knowing Babushka's state of health, Papa asked me not to miss any visits since he was unable to visit her while he was living "underground" in constant danger of arrest.

When we went for personal visits, I would bring food and cooking supplies to prepare homemade meals, hoping that Babushka's strength would be restored in at least a small way. During meals, the children would tell her funny stories about little Alex and what was happening in their school life. Babushka would also tell us something amusing, most often from her own childhood. She did not talk much about camp life in front of Lisa and Jane as it was too painful and not meant for children's ears.

After the children went to bed, she and I would talk about difficult matters. She told me how depressing everything was around her. Most of the elderly women in her barracks were murderers. Their hearts were so hardened that they did not want to hear even one word about God. The days were filled with their quarrels and swearing. A radio blared at full volume, and if someone asked to have it turned down a little, the only response would be harsh cursing.

With tears in her eyes Babushka told me about her heart pains and bladder infection and about the heartless doctor at the infirmary who only ridiculed her when she asked for help. "Prisoner Vins, why are you asking me to help you?" the doctor would say mockingly. "Let your God help you, if He exists! Go back to your barracks! I want nothing to do with you!"

As Babushka sat in front of me, so worn and pale and short of breath, my heart broke for her. But how could I help? More than once, I had tried to bring her medicine, but the doctor always refused to accept it.

Then Babushka would suggest that we pray. As we got down on our knees, an outcry for God's deliverance would come out of our hearts. After we prayed, I would try to cheer her up by telling her something happy and bright about our youth group. Babushka would come alive, asking about everyone because she had known my friends since we had been kids.

Once during such a midnight conversation she told me, "You know, Natasha, the Lord has a special way of comforting me. When I am discouraged and have no strength to go on, I have a recurring dream. After it, I always wake up with a feeling of happiness!

"I dream about the black soil in early spring, when the snow has just melted. The soil is soft and full of moisture. And then come the first green sprouts—young, fresh, full of life. When I wake up, such happiness fills my heart—life goes on! I start praising God for His goodness, for His help in everything. Bible verses come to mind, encouraging my heart that 'the sufferings of this present time are not worthy to be compared with the glory which shall be revealed in us,' Romans 8:18. And my all-time favorite: 'It is of the Lord's mercies that we are not consumed, because his compassions fail not. They are new every morning: great is thy faithfulness,' Lamentations 3:22, 23."

At the beginning of 1973 I had only one semester left before graduation, but problems started to develop when the administration of our college invited a special speaker to present an atheistic lecture. All the students and professors were gathered in the meeting hall. At first the lecturer spoke in general terms of how harmful religion is. But before long he proceeded to name specific names, including my father's and other pastors in Kiev. He slandered them, accusing them of being "anti-Soviet." Distorting the facts, the lecturer described some "horrible incidents" of supposed sectarian brutality.

Luba and I just looked at each other in disbelief, hearing such nonsense about people we knew well. Toward the end of the lecture he asked if anybody had questions. I raised my hand and began to question him on the "facts" he had presented. I mentioned that he was speaking about my father and other people I knew well.

"That's enough!" he tried to stop me. "I've heard a lot about you, Vins. Even in grade school you had a reputation as a zealous sectarian. I am not going to answer your questions!"

"Why don't you let her speak?" The girls from my class began protesting. "This is about her father, and she knows better than anyone what really happened."

Our director got up and ordered silence. Then she thanked the lecturer for such a substantial and interesting lecture and told us to return to our classrooms. Students surrounded me. "Natasha, tell us what really happened! We know that you and Luba believe in God, but we never heard about such atrocities."

The next day I was told to report to the director's office, where she was waiting with the assistant principal. The questioning began. "Where is your father? Is he hiding from prosecution? Is it true that your grandma is also in prison? What a shame to have such a family. Are you imagining that we will let you graduate? Remember, Natasha, religion and medicine are incompatible!" Frequent summons to the director's office continued for several weeks, but for the time being I was still allowed to attend classes.

The time had come for our next visit with Babushka. As always, I submitted a request to the administration office, asking for permission to miss two days of classes due to my family situation. I used to receive such permissions without any problem. But this time the assistant principal refused to authorize my request.

She called me in and asked, "What kind of family situation do you have?"

"My grandmother in prison camp is very ill. I must visit her."

"You are not going anywhere! I will not authorize your request."

I began imploring, trying to explain how difficult it was for Babushka in the camp and how much our visits meant to her. But the assistant principal was unrelenting, "No, I will not excuse you from classes for that reason."

I left her office feeling desperate about the situation. I knew that missing a visit with Babushka would be a tragedy for her. When I came home, one of Mama's friends who had stopped by for tea listened to my story. Then she made a suggestion, "I know a nurse who will sign a note excusing you from attending classes for health reasons." I agreed to that, thinking that even though this was not the best way to solve my problem, I just didn't know what else to do.

The visit with Babushka went well. I did not tell her about my problems, so she would not worry about me. When I returned home, a note signed by a nurse was waiting for me. The next day I submitted it to the administration office.

Two days later the assistant principal summoned me to her office. Her first words were, "So, now you are using fake medical excuses. That's very indecent, especially for a Christian. For that, we can expel you instantly!" I was silent, as I had nothing to say in my defense.

Another week passed. I was feeling anxious. Finally the assistant principal announced a special business meeting of our class. After many accusations she announced that the administration had decided to expel me.

"Why is she being expelled?" students started to object. "Can't you punish her in some other way? Like taking her scholarship away or giving her a warning? She is such a good student—and only three months are left before the final exams!"

The assistant principal did not appreciate their interference and abruptly stopped them. "This is final! Natasha has been already expelled."

I was crying. I felt ashamed before my classmates and especially before God because I was certainly at fault and now had to pay for my mistake. The girls surrounded me, saying, "Natasha, we will go straight to the director and beg her to reinstate you. This note from a nurse wasn't such a big deal. Some of us have done the same thing."

They selected several representatives to go see the director. But she would not even listen to them and repeated what the assistant principal already said—the decision was final.

I went home feeling hopeless. On one hand I knew that the nurse's note was just an excuse to expel me. The director had already given the main reason earlier. "So, you think we will let you graduate? Remember, Natasha, religion and medicine are incompatible!" On the other hand I had provided them with the excuse to expel me. But what should I do now? I had no other qualifications, and besides I liked nursing very much.

News was waiting for me at home. Papa was in Kiev and wanted to meet with me at the Dubinins' home. When it got dark, Lisa and I left home as if we were going to take a walk. For about half an hour we walked from street to street to make sure that no one followed us. Then we took a bus to the house where Papa was staying. The hostess led us to the room. Papa hugged Lisa and me. I was crying. He had already heard about my difficulties at college, but did not know yet that I had been expelled.

I told him everything: about the lecturer and what had followed, about my talks with the director and her declaration that religion and medicine are not compatible, and about how I had reached a dead end concerning my trip to see Babushka. I also told him the reaction of my classmates, who said, "Why is this note from a nurse such a big deal? Some of us have done it before."

Papa just listened, and when I finished he said, "Natasha, I understand how much you are hurting now. But I have to tell you how I see things. Of course, you were expelled because you are a Christian and because you belong to our family. At the same time you handed them a powerful weapon against yourself, and they used it. But this is only one side of the issue. Now let's discuss what you did by using a false notice. Natasha, it's dishonest! It does not matter that your classmates said many of them do similar things. For you this is not an excuse. You are a Christian, and that presents the highest responsibility."

I was still trying to justify myself even though in my heart I knew how wrong was what I had done. "Papa, but even Christians are doing such things! The lady who suggested that I take this note—"

"That's wrong thinking!" Papa interrupted. "You are responsible for your own actions and can't excuse yourself because others consider certain things acceptable. I am grateful to God that He didn't let you get away with it. Treasure this lesson, daughter, and remember it as long as you live. It alarms me when a Christian begins to think that everything is permissible. For me, Christian integrity is the highest treasure, and I am always cautious not to mar it."

16

With God's help, Babushka survived her term and was due for release on December 1, 1973. Mama and Peter went to the prison camp to meet her. At home, everything was ready for her return. Many Christian friends had gathered at our house to welcome her. When Babushka arrived, she could hardly believe that she was home again, resting in her own comfortable bedroom, enjoying the tender care of her family.

For the first time Babushka met two-year-old Alex, who was born while she was in prison, and they became fast friends. Her only sorrow was that she was not able to see her son. Because Papa was on the KGB's nationwide wanted list, our house was under constant surveillance, and he could not by any means come home.

Since Babushka was released just before Christmas, the holidays that year were especially brightened by her presence. Her health gradually improved after her return home. She valued each day of freedom and often told us what lessons she had learned being in a prison camp:

"At some distance from our camp were high-rise apartment buildings. In the evenings I liked to watch the windows as the lights were turned on. It was hard to believe that normal life was going on elsewhere. As I watched people come home from work and have their dinner with the whole family gathered around the table, I used to think, 'Will the day come for me too, when I will be able to walk outside the prison gates and go where I want to? Will I ever be able to lie down during the day when I am tired and want to take a nap without being shouted at by guards?'

"In prison I learned to value even the smallest blessings God provides in everyday life. Look at how much we have on the dinner table: all kinds of bread, vegetables, milk. In prison camp I used to wish for just one glass of milk. Sometimes at night I had hunger-dreams.

"A year before my prison term was up, I was ordered to appear before a parole committee. But the reality is, they don't release prisoners just because they are old and sick. They suggested that I write a statement saying I didn't believe in God anymore, and then they would let me go home. I told them, 'I am an old woman. It would be dishonorable if at the end of my life I did something like that just to gain freedom!' They replied, 'Very well, then you will have to finish your term!' So, with God's help I did finish my term. And now I am home, endlessly grateful to the Lord for His mercy and protection in those years. I learned in prison not to worry about tomorrow, but to place my everyday trials in God's hands."

Soon after Babushka's release I began experiencing difficulties at work. At the time I was working as a physical therapist at a hospital for children with bone tuberculosis. In January the head doctor called me into his office. Two other hospital administrators were there. As soon as I entered his office, the head doctor began yelling at me, saying that I was from a dissident family, that my father was evading arrest, and that I, too, was a sectarian. He demanded that I quit my job at the hospital.

Once again, just like the time I was expelled from the nursing college, I was told that religion and medicine were incompatible. At the end of his tirade, the head doctor suggested that I write a letter of resignation. I objected that I did not wish to quit because I liked my job.

"You will be sorry for this," he began threatening me. "I will find a reason to fire you!"

In a few weeks I was fired 'due to a reduction in staff,' even though our hospital was experiencing shortages in physical therapists and nurses at the time.

After Papa found out that I lost my job, he sent one of his "underground" co-workers with a message to me. He suggested that before I got another job, I come and help him for a couple of months, which I was happy to do. With many precautions, his co-worker escorted me to the city where Papa was at the moment. When we met, Papa told me about the project I would be working on.

The underground printing house, called "The Christian," was getting ready to publish a hymnbook in the Ukrainian language. About four hundred hymns had to be selected out of several old hymnbooks. To do that, someone had to travel to Western Ukraine and work for several weeks with the choir directors compiling the list. Katya, a worker of the printing house, was in charge of this project.

My task was to assist Katya in this assignment. Every Saturday choir directors from several towns would gather for the entire day to work with Katya, while I prepared meals for everybody, set the table, and did the dishes. Between Saturdays I helped Katya type up the hymns that had already been chosen for the hymnbook.

Three weeks later Katya had to take a break and go to Moscow for a few days. She wanted me to go with her. Papa happened to be in Moscow, and I was glad to spend a couple of days with him. The morning after our arrival, he was scheduled to meet a pastor from a different city who was passing through Moscow. When Papa and I arrived at the prearranged meeting place, it turned out that the pastor would be three or four hours late. We couldn't wait in that apartment and had to pass the time just walking the streets of Moscow.

That day in early March was gloomy and windy, with piles of snow still on the ground, even though the temperature was above freezing. As we walked and walked along the sidewalks, trying to avoid the puddles, Papa and I had a good talk about things that concerned us. It was evident that sooner or later a long prison term awaited him. In light of it we discussed the future of our family; we talked about the younger kids, Mama, and Babushka. Papa shared with me some of the challenges in ministry he was experiencing at the moment.

As he noticed that I was shivering in the cold wind, he suggested we stop at a local supermarket and get a cup of coffee to warm up. We did, and then went back outside and continued walking. Papa encouraged me not to be anxious about his arrest. He emphasized that the greatest value in his life was faithfulness to God and to biblical teaching. He talked about his own father, who was killed in prison for the "crime" of preaching the gospel. I appreciated every moment of our talk.

The next day Katya and I left for Ukraine to finish the work on the hymnbook. Papa, too, was supposed to leave for the Urals and Siberia to visit the secret printing teams. On the overnight train my thoughts kept going back to my last few days in Moscow. I thanked God for arranging everything: Papa being there right at that time, the unexpected delay, and our long conversation on that cold, windy day. My main impression of our talk was of how profoundly Papa trusted God. I felt that even if he were arrested again, I would not despair because of what I got to know about him during our last talk.

In the beginning of April, Katya and I finished with the hymnbook and were ready to return to Moscow. The next step was to deliver the selected hymns to the typesetter. Papa was supposed to be back from Siberia at about the same time. I wanted to see him once again before I returned to Kiev to get a job.

Our train arrived in Moscow after dark. All the passengers had their coats on and their suitcases ready. As always at the end of such trips, Katya and I were anxious that the KGB agents would not notice us. Train stations, especially in a big city like Moscow, were the most dangerous places. The secret police constantly watched the passengers. I prayed silently, "Lord, only You can protect us. You promised in Your Word to guard our coming in and going out. I trust Your power and strength."

When the train stopped, Katya and I stepped down to the platform. Bypassing the train station building, we went to the subway stop. When we arrived at the high-rise apartment building we were looking for, Katya rang the doorbell. As we entered, Maria, our hostess, greeted us. "Come in! Welcome! Thank God for your safe arrival!"

My first question was, "Is Papa already here?"

"No, he is not back yet. Three people are already waiting for him. He promised to be back no later than the fifth. But don't worry; he will be back soon. Something urgent probably delayed him. Such things have happened before. But why are we standing by the door? Take your coats off and come in."

As we walked into the room, several members of the secret printing team surrounded us. "Natasha! Katya! How was your trip? Georgi Petrovich* was supposed to be here by now. We are waiting for him."

Our hostess walked into the room, "Let's pray and thank God for His protection for Katya and Natasha as they traveled." After we prayed, she invited us all to have dinner.

The life of the family in this apartment was quite unusual. On the one hand, everything seemed rather ordinary. Each morning the father left for work, the children went to school, and the mother stayed home. However, often the doorbell would ring, Maria would open the door, and in would come people who had to stay in the farthest room of the apartment, and with whom the family members spoke only in hushed voices. The children were not allowed to mention to any outsider that someone was staying with them. This family alone knew and guarded the secrets of God's underground workers. Even the youngest child in the family understood the seriousness of the situation.

The next morning the doorbell woke us up early. Katya whispered, "It's Georgi Petrovich!" But it was not him. Another worker from the publishing house had come at the appointed date to consult with Papa. We were beginning to worry but at the same time tried not to lose hope, comforting each other that this was probably a simple delay. Something urgent had probably come up, and he had to take an unexpected detour before returning to Moscow.

The next day Pastor Minyakov and Victor arrived. After considering the situation, they decided that it was time to do something. Victor was asked to fly to Chelyabinsk, Papa's final destination in the Ural Mountains, and try to find out what had happened. As for the rest of us, the only thing to do was wait. The days dragged on and on. We spent time in prayer. Our shared concerns brought us closer to each other.

---

*Friends use the name "Petrovich," which literally meant "son of Peter." This is the respectful way of addressing an older man.

During those days of somber waiting, I was thinking over every word, every detail of my last talk with Papa. Only three weeks had passed since that day. Papa had said to me then, "Natasha, how much I enjoy our time of sharing! How many times I wished I could spend time with my father. I missed him a lot growing up. I used to imagine that we would meet and just talk, talk, talk. As a teenager I needed his advice. I wanted to ask him some vital questions. But I saw him for the last time when I was eight. Natasha, you are twenty-one already. Even if I get arrested again and my life ends in prison, nobody will be able to deprive you of your memories of growing up knowing your father."

Several days later Victor returned and told us what he had learned in the Urals. Papa had arrived there safely, had met with the ministers in Chelyabinsk, and on March 30 they saw him off at the train station. His destination was Novosibirsk. Two days later the police conducted house searches in the homes of many Christians in Chelyabinsk. They were acting on orders from the prosecutor's office in Kiev "in connection with Georgi Vins's criminal case." That left no doubt that Papa was arrested on his way to Novosibirsk.

We all got on our knees and prayed for God's special mercy for him. For me it was comforting that I learned the news of his arrest in a circle of his devoted friends who had shared with him all the dangers of the underground ministry in recent years. Just as he was, each one of them was at risk of being imprisoned. I felt that his arrest brought as much pain to their hearts as to mine.

Now I felt urgency to return home, even though Victor let me know that the pastor in Chelyabinsk had already sent a messenger to give the news to our family. I arrived home the day after Easter. There, Lisa told me some exciting news. Late on Saturday night, before Easter Sunday, about twenty young people from our youth group had gone to the prison walls and sang "Christ Is Risen" for Papa. But since nobody knew where his cell was, they were not sure he heard them.[*]

---

[*]Lukyanovskaya Prison was a huge, century-old prison built in the time of the czars long ago. It encompassed a whole city block.

They were able to sing only one hymn before the prison guards appeared and chased them away.

Later Papa told us his side of the story. "Four of us were in a cell. It was quite late, and everyone was asleep. Then suddenly in my sleep I heard singing: 'Christ is risen!' I wasn't fully awake and for a brief moment thought that I was already in heaven, that prison and sufferings were left behind! An incredible happiness filled my heart. But as the singing grew louder, I fully awoke and understood that young voices were singing outside the window. The words of the Easter hymn filled our cell. Everyone woke up, exclaiming in bewilderment, 'Listen! Listen!' Other prisoners were tapping on the walls; the whole prison was awake.

"Suddenly we heard the barking of guard dogs and the shouting of guards. The singing ceased. Then I understood—my Christian friends had decided to encourage me in such a unique way. But I was still puzzled. How did they know which cell I was in? It seemed like they were singing right under my window!"

17

Seven months had passed since Papa's arrest. It was already the end of October, and we had not received any news from him. Our home life proceeded as usual. I got a job as a lab technician at the medical center, Lisa was in seventh grade, Jane in third, and little Alex was almost three years old. Peter, after graduating from high school, wanted to continue his education, but was denied entrance to college. While still in high school, Peter was approached by KGB agents with a proposal to collaborate with them and report on his father. In return the KGB promised to grant him admission to the university. Of course, Peter refused to have any association with the KGB.

Almost a year had passed since Babushka's release from prison camp. Her health had improved considerably, and she once again was actively involved in the ministry of the Council of Prisoners' Relatives. She was anxious about Papa. Having just served three years of imprisonment herself, she could clearly picture what he was going through. Papa's case was handled by Investigator Bekh, the same man who handled Babushka's case when she had been arrested four years earlier.

One October evening the doorbell rang at our house. When Mama opened the door, she saw a policeman. She was relieved that he was alone, which meant that the purpose of his visit was not a house search. He handed Mama a notice to appear at the prosecutor's office at nine o'clock the next morning. Mama was concerned and asked the policeman, "Has something happened to my husband?" He did not know and said he was merely ordered to deliver the notice.

The following morning Mama, Babushka, Peter, and I went to the prosecutor's office. Investigator Bekh immediately announced, "Two of you will go into Lukyanovksaya Prison with me to see Georgi Petrovich. Go there right away. I'll meet you by the prison entrance."

We looked at each other, perplexed. What was the meaning of this? Usually the family was not allowed to see a prisoner before the trial.

"What's going on? Is Georgi sick?" Babushka asked Bekh.

"No. The investigation is completed, and his case is going to court. Georgi Petrovich needs a defense attorney. He wants to discuss with his family which attorney to hire for his trial."

We were astonished. Christians put on trial usually refused to accept an attorney, since all the attorneys in the USSR were atheists and would collaborate with the prosecution rather than attempt to defend their Christian clients. During his first trial in 1966, Papa refused to get an attorney. It made no sense that now he would want to discuss hiring an attorney. Even more astonishing was that the KGB allowed him this visit with his family before the trial.

We left the prosecutor's office and took a bus to Lukyanovskaya prison. On the way there we decided that since only two of us were allowed to see Papa, Mama and Babushka should go. Peter and I would wait outside. Bekh was already at the entrance, and they followed him inside.

About twenty minutes later Mama and Babushka came out. We rushed towards them. "How's Papa? What's going on with him?"

"He doesn't look well and seems exhausted," Mama said. "He sent you greetings and was so sorry that you were not allowed to see him!"

"So, what was decided about getting an attorney?" Peter asked.

Babushka replied, "Let me start at the very beginning. As we entered, Bekh walked in front of us. Nadia and I followed him down into the basement. And there, Georgi was already waiting in a small office. I was happy to see him again; this was our first meeting in four years!

"Bekh warned us, 'Your visit will be brief and to the point. Georgi Petrovich has agreed to hire an attorney. Now he will tell you whom he has chosen. I will record everything that is discussed here.'

" 'Georgi, I can't believe you decided to hire an attorney,' Nadia said.

" 'I have seriously considered it and decided to get an attorney this time.' Georgi responded. 'I want you to appeal to Christian organizations in the West to find me a Christian attorney.'

"Bekh almost jumped off his chair and indignantly shouted, 'Vins, how dare you make such a statement! You know perfectly well that the whole idea of getting an attorney from abroad is ridiculous. The authorities will never let you do it! You are a deceiver! You asked for a meeting with your family to discuss the issue of attorney. But I see now that you didn't have any intention of doing it; you just wanted to see your mother and wife!'

" 'That's not true.' Georgi protested. 'I studied the court documents, and all the accusations against me are of a religious nature. Even our Baptist doctrines are under attack. Therefore an atheist attorney will not be competent in those issues. And as far as I know, there are no Christian attorneys in the Soviet Union.'

"Bekh quickly began writing all this down. Georgi continued to advise Nadia and me, 'As soon as you get the name of an attorney who agrees to participate in my trial, you will have to appeal to the Ministry of Foreign Affairs with a request to allow him and his interpreter to come to the Soviet Union and get acquainted with my case.'

"After Bekh was done with recording the main points of our discussion, he asked each of us to sign the record. Then he signed it himself and announced that the visit was over. Georgi asked him, 'Would you please permit my mother to pray and give me her motherly blessing?' To our surprise, Bekh nodded. We stood up, and I prayed, asking for God's protection at the trial and during all the years in bonds that were ahead for Georgi. Then we hugged, said our good-byes, and parted."

Through some foreign tourists Mama was able to request a Christian attorney from abroad. Soon an answer came from Pastor Eugene Foss in Switzerland. He informed us "that a Christian attorney from Norway, Doctor of Law Alf Gerem, had agreed to travel to the Soviet Union and be Georgi Vins's defense attorney during his trial."

As soon as we got this news, Mama wrote a petition to Mr. Gromyko, the Minister of Foreign Affairs, requesting that Dr. Alf Gerem be permitted to enter the Soviet Union. A reply from the government officials never came back. But after all, that was not surprising since all the previous petitions our family had sent in the past years had always been ignored.

18

Papa's trial began on January 27, 1975. As usual, our family wasn't notified of when and where it would take place. Under the supervision of the KGB, a small courthouse on the outskirts of Kiev was selected. It was located on a side street that dead-ended against the fence of a military zone. Quite unexpectedly, just one day before the trial, we were able to find out the date and place.

On Monday morning I asked my supervisor at work for a few days off and went to the courthouse. When I located the right building, I found several policemen guarding the entrance. On the other side of the street I noticed a small group of Christians waiting. Mama, Babushka, and Peter were not among them, and I assumed that they were already inside. I walked up to a police officer, showed him my passport as proof that I was the daughter of a person on trial, and asked him to let me into the court. He answered that his orders were to not let anybody into the building until a recess.

I crossed the street to join my Christian friends. They were mostly elderly members of our church. They surrounded me, explaining that not one of them was allowed to enter the court building. Even Mama, Babushka, and Peter—the family members—had had a hard time getting in. However, quite a few strangers entered after showing passes.

The police officer had ordered the Christians to move away from the door to the opposite side of the street. So there we stood, waiting for a recess. All of us were anxious about what was going on in the courtroom. Polya, an elderly Christian lady, suggested that we pray. As we bowed our heads, several people prayed out loud. It started to snow and was bitterly cold. Someone discovered that there was a drugstore around the corner, and we took turns going in to warm up.

As the hours slipped by, I wondered why these elderly Christians did not go home. Why would they remain here all day in freezing weather if it was obvious that they would not be allowed into the courtroom? But they seemed quite determined to stay till the end of the day when the court session would be over, and I realized how lonely our family would feel without their sympathetic eyes and warm smiles.

Finally around lunchtime the front door opened, and out came Mama and Babushka. They began telling us their first impressions. Papa was handling it well, was composed and alert. When Judge Dyshel explained to him the rights of a defendant, Papa requested that the court-appointed attorney be dismissed. He based his request on the fact that all the accusations against him were of a religious nature and that the atheist-attorney was incompetent to deal with them. The attorney agreed with the defendant and left the courtroom.

Then the judge suggested proceeding without a defense attorney.

"No, I would not agree to that," Papa objected. "I asked my family to hire a Christian attorney to defend me at this trial."

Judge Dyshel asked Mama for an explanation. She answered, "Since all attorneys in the Soviet Union are atheists, we have invited a Christian attorney from Norway. Doctor of Law Alf Gerem has agreed to defend Georgi during the trial. Our family sent a telegram to Mr. Gromyko, the Minister of Foreign Affairs, requesting that he grant a visa to Dr. Gerem. However, our friends from Europe informed us that Dr. Gerem was denied a visa by the Soviet Embassy in Norway." Upon hearing this, Papa suggested that the trial be postponed until his attorney was permitted to attend. The judge denied the motion.

Mama had hardly finished telling us her story when the recess was over. This time I was allowed to go inside. The courtroom was large, seating about one hundred people. There were no empty seats, since the room was filled with KGB agents who carried entry passes. In addition to the five members of our family, only two elderly Christians were allowed into the courtroom. The following day, after some Christian witnesses had testified, they were also permitted to remain in the courtroom.

As we entered, Papa nodded and smiled. Even though our seats were not far from the defendant's bench where Papa sat flanked by two armed soldiers, we were not allowed to talk. But just being able to look at him was enough for me. I had not seen him for nearly a year, since that memorable last talk he and I had had as we walked along the streets of Moscow. Looking into his eyes, I tried to understand what was going on in his heart. But suddenly I realized that the court session had started and I had to listen carefully.*

Judge: Does the defendant have any petitions to the court?

Georgi Vins: Yes. I request to conduct a new analysis of all the religious literature connected to my case, since the previous pre-trial examination was biased, having been conducted by atheistic experts. Therefore, I insist that a Christian-based scientific analysis be conducted. At the time of my arrest, my briefcase contained, along with other Christian books, the manuscript for my new book. It contains biographies of church leaders Nikolai Odinstov, Pavel Datsko, Vasiliy Ivanov-Klyshnikov, and Georgi Shipkov. They were arrested for their Christian ministries several decades ago. All died in prison, and all were posthumously exonerated after the death of Stalin.

    The atheistic experts that analyzed my manuscript for this court concluded that my stories contain slander against the Soviet regime. I ask the court to request from the archives of the Supreme Court of the USSR and the Committee on Religious Affairs

---

*At the end of each day of the trial as many details as possible were written down of what was going on in the courtroom. These notes were later given to the Council of Prisoners' Relatives to be published in their "Prisoner Bulletin."

the documents concerning their exoneration. I would like this data to be announced here. I want to know on what basis these posthumously exonerated church leaders are classified by the atheistic experts as criminals.

Judge: (interrupting) Is that all, Vins?

Georgi Vins: No. I want the court to request from the Central Office of the Public Prosecution the total number of Christians sentenced for their religious beliefs from the year 1929 to the present, as well as the number of religious books confiscated all over the country during house searches: Bibles, New Testaments, hymnbooks, and other Christian books and magazines, from the year 1929 to the present. I also request information from the Ministry of Finances concerning the total amount of fines that officials exacted from Christians for conducting worship services, starting from 1961 to January of 1975.

Judge: Is that all, defendant Vins?

Georgi Vins: No, not all. But I can present the remaining petitions to you in writing.

The court secretary took the list of petitions from the defendant and handed them to the judge. After examining the list, the court denied all the requests of the defendant. In response the defendant proposed the court call a mistrial, since his defense attorney, Dr. Alf Gerem, was not allowed to come to the Soviet Union and participate in the trial, and of course, the court denied all his petitions, which were directly related to the trial procedure.

Judge Dyshel refused to call a mistrial and announced that the trial would continue as scheduled. The defendant then let the court know that in view of what had just happened he had no confidence in this court, and therefore declined to participate in the trial.

The judge then read the formal charges. The document was long, recorded on many pages. It took forty minutes to read it. After that the court announced a recess until the following morning.

The judge and two peoples' deputies—the jury—left the court-room first; then the guards led Papa out. As if on cue, the people that filled the courtroom burst into activity, talking loudly and bustling around. A group of men surrounded us, yelling insults addressed at our family. We felt so outnumbered and defenseless. It seemed that the "wheels of government" were going to crush us with ease. Our only desire at that moment was to flee the courtroom, to get out on the street where our friends were waiting.

As we left the court building, it was already getting dark, and the streetlights were shining. Across the street, instead of twenty elderly ladies we saw a large crowd of Christians. Almost the entire church had showed up, over two hundred people. Friends surrounded us, asking what was going on in the courtroom and how Papa was doing. Our elderly pastor, Efim Kovalenko, asked for silence. The crowd bowed their heads, and he prayed aloud, asking the Lord to give Papa courage and wisdom.

Babushka was so exhausted after such an intense day that she could hardly stand. She leaned on Peter's arm for support. Someone flagged down a taxi for us, and finally we were on our way home. When we rang the doorbell, Galina, a close friend of our family, opened the door. When she heard that the trial had started that morning, she took a week of vacation and came to our house to look after little Alex and Jane. Galina helped Babushka take her coat off and invited us to sit down for dinner.

The table was already set. For a moment I felt like a guest in my own house, which was an unusual feeling. But Galina insisted that she did not need any help in the kitchen. Everything was done and ready to be served.

"You've had such a difficult and stressful day," she said with a comforting smile, as she poured the steaming soup into our bowls. "Now it's time to relax. Let's eat, and then I want to hear your stories about the trial."

As I listened to her calm voice, it was hard to hold back the tears. God's loving-kindness and care were evident in the simple act of such a warm reception.

"Hast thou not known? hast thou not heard, that the everlasting God, the Lord, the Creator of the ends of the earth, fainteth not, neither is weary? there is no searching of his understanding. He giveth power to the faint; and to them that have no might he increaseth strength" (Isaiah 40:28–29).

19

Over the next three days the prosecuting attorney presented his evidence. He questioned the literary experts concerning the books and articles that Papa had with him on the day of his arrest. Also, dozens of witnesses were called to testify and were cross-examined by Judge Dyshel and Prosecutor Tsekhotsky. After questioning each witness, the judge would ask the accused if he had any questions. Papa's answer was always the same, "Yes, I have questions for the witness. But I will ask them only in the presence of my attorney, Dr. Alf Gerem."

The complete lack of impartiality and fairness on the part of the experts, the judge, and the prosecutor was stunning. They had no desire to clarify the evidence or to find out what the circumstances were really like. The trial procedure left an impression that the verdict had been reached long in advance, before the trial had even started, and that now an orchestrated farce of total lawlessness was unfolding in front of us.

One of the accusations against Papa was a brief message he had preached at the wedding of two church members, Vasily and Vera Shuportyak, on August 24, 1969. The witnesses claimed in court that Vins's message contained "anti-Soviet" statements and an incitement to disobey the law. The indictment even stated that "the marriage was in fact fictitious, as the sectarians wished to use the pretext of a wedding to gather for an illegal meeting, which was attended by five hundred people."

Neither Vasily nor Vera Shuportyak was asked to testify at the trial. Vera came to the court and requested to be a witness. Judge Dyshel agreed. Vera presented their family photograph with two young sons and a baby daughter, along with the birth certificates of the children to prove that the wedding ceremony was genuine. While answering the judge's and the prosecutor's questions, Vera testified that Georgi Vins's sermon at her wedding did not contain any appeals to disobey the law, but had a purely biblical message.

> Judge: Witness Shuportyak, nobody is asking you to make conclusions. Answer only the questions you are asked! We have a tape with Georgi Vins's message. The experts have listened to it and concluded that it contains calls to disobey Soviet law.
>
> Vera: Then the experts are mistaken. I suggest that we listen to this tape now. It's only half an hour long. You will hear for yourself what the message was about.
>
> Judge: We don't need to listen to the tape. It is sufficient to know what our experts have concluded in this matter. Witness Shuportyak, step down; I don't have any more questions for you.
>
> Vera: But you are deciding the destiny of a man here! You are ready to sentence him to a long prison term, and Georgi Vins has five children. You are dooming them to a childhood without a father! Isn't this a valid reason to try to be objective and listen to the tape?
>
> Judge: I have already told you to step down, Witness Shuportyak! We don't have any more questions for you. Do you wish the guards to escort you out of the courtroom?

This was the kind of atmosphere that prevailed during all five days of the trial. While interrogating a young Christian woman, Lena Mashnitsky, the judge began to ridicule her, making sarcastic comments on her replies to the prosecutor. Papa sharply interrupted him, "Who gave you the right to mock her Christian faith?"

On the fourth day Prosecutor Tsekhotsky concluded his arguments and demanded that Georgi Vins be sentenced to ten years of imprisonment with the confiscation of his personal property. Even though we had expected that the sentence would be harsh, the substance of the prosecutor's speech seemed especially cruel.

> Judge: Vins, you are now granted a chance to say something in your own defense.

> Georgi Vins: It is the task of my lawyer, Dr. Alf Gerem, to defend me during this trial. Since he was not allowed to participate in my trial, I am not going to defend myself. I place my defense in the hands of my Lord Jesus Christ!

> Judge: That's up to you. And now, according to the law, you are allowed to make your final statement.

> Georgi Vins: The final statement on my behalf at this trial I will also leave with my Lord, who is the Alpha and Omega, the Beginning and the End, the First and the Last!

The judge announced that the verdict would be read on the following day and dismissed us. We made our way out of the court building. It was growing dark outside. About two hundred Christians were gathered on the street some distance from the courthouse. We told them the news of the prosecutor's demand to sentence Papa to ten years of imprisonment. Everybody was stunned by the news.

Suddenly someone exclaimed, "Look! They brought the police car to the main entrance. And they are leading Brother Vins to it!" Suddenly the whole crowd of Christians surged toward the police car. This happened so unexpectedly that the policemen who were guarding the street and the courthouse did not have a chance to stop the crowd.

We stood six or seven feet away from the vehicle, overflowing the sidewalks and the road. The other end of the street was a dead end, so the police car could not get away. Somebody began singing a hymn, and everyone joined in, but after the first few words the singing ceased as many of us were crying. But we had to overcome our emotions and continue singing since our prisoner needed encouragement. So, at first just a few voices and then the whole crowd carried on the hymn.

Policemen were yelling at us, demanding that we disperse and let the vehicle pass. But they could not do much against such a huge crowd. We sang a couple more hymns and about ten minutes later moved away, letting the police car pass. My heart rejoiced as I imagined how our singing had encouraged Papa after the prosecutor's harsh speech.

Later on Papa described his impressions, "After the prosecutor pronounced the indictment, the guards led me to the police car to take me back to prison. As I sat there in the dark, I suddenly heard singing. One of the guards said to me, 'They are singing for you.' The guards were smiling. I remember that the car tried to pull away but abruptly stopped again. And I sat there and listened to our Christian hymns.

"I was especially encouraged by the hymn 'Vorkuta.' This well-known hymn was written by a Christian prisoner and is full of hope that the Lord will not forsake His servants. 'The handcuffs will fall down, the chains will be broken! Christ's warriors will gain freedom! They will become empowered by the Spirit and will take the words of Truth to the nations!' The words of this hymn were ringing in my heart all the way to prison."

The verdict was pronounced the following day. The members of our family, plus Vera Shuportyak and other Christian witnesses who were allowed in the courtroom, brought fresh roses and carnations hidden under our coats. Everyone had to stand while the verdict was read. It lasted for an hour. Once again, as in the indictment, different facts were listed and presented in a way that would endorse the articles of the Criminal Code.

I looked at Papa. He stood facing the window while the verdict was read, looking at the gray winter sky. I was amazed at the deep calm that I could see on his face. Finally, the judge declared, "Georgi Vins is being sentenced to five years of prison camps plus five years of Siberian exile, with the confiscation of his personal property."

"Do you understand the verdict?" he addressed the accused.

"Yes. Let the Lord's name be praised!" Papa answered.

Suddenly pandemonium broke out. KGB agents began to clap and stamp their feet, shouting, "This was a fair trial! He got what he deserved!" Others yelled, "He didn't get enough! He should be sentenced to life!" All this noise and the angry outcries gave a disheartening feeling of unbridled lawlessness.

At that moment Peter threw flowers to Papa, shouting, "Papa, this is for your courage!" The rest of us likewise began throwing Papa flowers. Mama shouted, "Georgi, you won this case!"

The guards led Papa through the courtroom to the door. He carried our flowers in his hands. When he walked by me, I exclaimed, "With Christ there is freedom even in prison!"

A KGB agent who stood near me hissed, "What a fanatic! All of you should rot in prison!"

20

After the trial we were allowed a thirty-minute visit with Papa in prison. He had no idea where he would be transported to prison camp. One of the guards hinted that his destination would be the far north, and Papa asked us to bring him warm clothes. Mama brought him a care package with some food and winter clothes. A month later, when he was due for another parcel, she was told that prisoner Vins was no longer in the Kiev prison. He was somewhere in transit to his new location.

Finally a letter arrived from Yakutsk with the address of his camp. Peter unrolled a map of the Soviet Union, and we found Yakutsk. It was in the far north, many thousands of miles from Kiev. The only way to get there was by airplane. Mama and Peter set out to visit Papa. His camp was located in the small town of Tabaga, thirty kilometers from Yakutsk.

That summer I found myself at a crossroads. I was already twenty-two years old and had to make some choices concerning my direction in life. The church leaders asked me to consider full-time Christian service with the underground printing house "The Christian." This was the opportunity of a lifetime! The ministry of secretly printing Bibles, New Testaments, hymnals, Christian magazines, and children's materials held a strong appeal for me. In our atheistic country, where all Christian books were confiscated and destroyed, I could see no higher calling than to help fill that need. Another strong attraction for me lay in the fact that Papa had been greatly involved with underground printing before his arrest.

Even though my pastor encouraged my inclination for full-time Christian service, Mama and Babushka firmly refused to let me go and live "underground."* They said, "We already have enough worries for one family to deal with! Papa has been imprisoned for ten years and sent to a camp far away from home. Now you also would become a candidate for prison, living in danger until you are arrested somewhere. No, that's just too much. We need you at home." I tried to persuade them that I was old enough to follow my own calling in life, but nothing could change their minds.

I was strongly convinced that God was leading me to this ministry but didn't feel free to leave home against the wishes of my family. I suggested that we pray about it and wait till the next visit with Papa to ask for his opinion. Our next visit was scheduled for November. I prayed a lot before that trip to Yakutsk since the decision to be made there would affect the direction of my life.

Upon our arrival at the camp, we were aware that listening devices had been planted in our room. Therefore I wrote Papa a note on a piece of paper about my desire to be a part of the printing ministry. As soon as he read it, Papa burned the note. He wasn't ready to answer me right away, but wanted to think and pray about it and to discuss it with Mama.

The next morning he wrote me his response.

> I am glad that you consider God's work the most important in your life. Mama expressed her fears, and I partly agree with her. For me, too, it would be very painful if you are ever arrested. But how can I say "No!" if you are convinced that the Lord has put this desire in your heart?

> My dear girl, I give you my blessing! Serve the Lord, Natasha, and remember that you will always be in my prayers.

Soon after that I left home. A totally unfamiliar way of life began with new friends, new surroundings, and the strict discipline of "underground" living. I was learning how crucial personal responsibility

---

*In order to be involved in such a ministry in the Soviet Union, a person had to leave his hometown and become a part of the "underground" printing operation, hiding from arrest.

for my actions was. Even minor carelessness could lead to the arrest of friends and the confiscation of books that were printed in such risky conditions. In a fresh new way I began to see the reality of God's help and protection. The years of underground ministry became an overwhelming school of life.

In those days we secretly delivered Christian books in our suitcases, traveling by train to the remotest parts of the country. There were many delivery teams. Ours consisted of three—sometimes four—people. We would pack our bags to the limit of our ability to carry them. Before leaving for the train station, we earnestly prayed for God's protection so that all the literature could be safely delivered.

At times, when the train was approaching a station where we needed to get off, other passengers would volunteer to help carry our luggage to the exit. We tried to avoid this, since the weight of our suitcases could raise suspicions. Once when it was impossible to refuse the assistance of a helpful passenger, the man exclaimed after lifting one of the bags, "Girls, have you lost your minds? You are going to break your backs! What do you have in there? Bricks?" At that moment we could only silently ask God to restrain any suspicions this person might have and to help us get off the train safely.

After getting off, we would walk down the tracks to the nearest bus stop, bypassing the train station building where KGB agents were on duty. Our heavy suitcases might attract their attention, and we could be in danger of a search. When we finally reached our destination, we would be completely exhausted by the heavy bags and several days of traveling.

But what awaited us at the end of our journey would take away the fatigue and inspire us to continue this work. As we unloaded Bibles, New Testaments, and children's books from our suitcases, we would see the tears of joy in the eyes of the pastor and his wife and hear their prayers of thanksgiving. This was the greatest reward we could receive. The pastor would share with us how many needs these books would fill, not only in his church, but also in the surrounding towns and villages where they would be distributed.

Then we would be invited to the dinner table. As we shared a meal with the pastor's family, our host would tell us about the blessings and hardships that his church was experiencing. He would also ask us about the lives of believers in other cities we had visited while delivering Bibles.

After dinner we would finally have a chance to take a shower and do some personal laundry. That night, we would enjoy sleeping in real beds instead of on a bench on the train; the floor beneath us would not be vibrating, and we did not hear the clicking sound of train wheels on rails.

In the morning the road awaited us once again. Train stations, heavy suitcases, buses, train cars—this was our destiny month after month, year after year.

21

The first half of Papa's ten-year sentence ended on March 31, 1979, but he still had to serve five years of exile somewhere in a village in Siberia. As a rule, families were allowed to join prisoners in exile. Back home, we were getting ready to travel as soon as he let us know his new location. We packed several large suitcases with blankets, towels, warm clothes, and dishes, since basic supplies were scarce in the remote regions of Siberia.

We were quite concerned that we had not heard from Papa for over two months. His last letter had come in February. In April Mama sent a telegram to the camp administrator: "We are worried about the life of Georgi Vins. Let us know where he is."

An answer came back: "Prisoner Vins is in transit to Tyumen, Siberia."

Two more weeks passed, and still there was no word from Papa. Mama decided to go to Siberia to search for him.

Tuesday, April 24, Tyumen

Mama arrived in Tyumen late in the afternoon and went straight from the airport to the local prison. When she handed a package for Papa to the guard, he took it and disappeared behind the plywood partition. Finally, the guard came out to the waiting room and announced, "Prisoner Vins is allowed to receive a package. Are you his wife?"

Mama nodded, her heart racing with joy. "Thank you, Lord, that I found Georgi on the first try."

"May I see my husband?" she asked the guard.

"I don't know about that. You have to ask the warden."

"How do I go about seeing the warden?"

"It's already too late. Come back tomorrow at 10:00 A.M."

Wednesday, April 25, Tyumen

After spending the night in a motel, Mama went to the regional prison headquarters to find out where Papa would be exiled. The administrator checked the papers and informed her that prisoner Vins would spend his exile in the Tyumen region, in the village of Berezovo. Mama asked him when her husband would be taken there. He replied, "In about two or three weeks. As soon as the ice melts on the Tobol River, the prisoners will be transported north on a barge."

From the regional prison headquarters Mama went back to the local prison. The warden signed a permit for a visit. When the guard walked Mama into the meeting room, Papa was already there. A thick glass barrier separated them. The guard gestured toward a telephone receiver. She noticed that Papa had already put his own phone up to his ear. As they started to say hello into the receivers, an unfamiliar voice interrupted them, "First listen to the rules of the visit!" It turned out that an officer at the other end of the room had a third receiver. He warned them that he would be monitoring their conversation.

When they could finally talk, Papa said, "Nadia, what a surprise! How did you find out that I was in Tyumen? I couldn't write home since no letters are allowed in transit."

"The warden in Tabaga informed us that you were sent to Tyumen."

"Thank God! You can't imagine how special your visit is. The conditions here are awful. I am in a transit cell which is badly over-crowded. Some of us have to sleep on the cement floor. Everything is dirty and full of lice. It's just unbearable!"

"I am so sorry! But I have some news for you. Just this morning I went to the prison headquarters, and they told me that you will be transported farther north to a small village called Berezovo."

"But when? I was supposed to be in my place of exile three weeks ago. Every extra day in my cell is torture."

"They will transport you sometime in May, when the river is clear of ice."

The visit lasted only thirty minutes. Mama returned to the airport to begin her long journey back home, and Papa went back to his over-crowded cell, uplifted by this short visit. He was thinking about his exile and the arrival of the family. He tried to imagine what life would be like in a Siberian village. He had some concerns that the children would have a hard time adjusting to a primitive hut with an outhouse and other inconveniences, but he comforted himself that somehow they would make it. What mattered most was that the family would be together again.

Thursday, April 26, Tyumen

Right after breakfast the next morning the guard opened the door to the cell. "Vins, pick up your things and step out!" he shouted.

Papa grabbed his bag, thinking, "At last I am on my way to exile!" But then a troubling thought came. "Why is it just me? Why are no others called for the transport?"

The guard led him to the warden's office. Two other officers were there.

"Prisoner Vins, I have received an urgent order to transport you to Moscow. These two officers will accompany you," the warden announced.

"Go to Moscow? But why?"

"My duty is to follow the orders I receive. I don't have any explanation. Right now you will be taken directly to the airport."

All this was so disturbing! What was going on? Papa's thoughts were racing. "Exile is usually served in Siberia, as far from home as possible. Why are they transporting me to Moscow all of a sudden? Perhaps some other Baptist ministers were arrested, and now I am going to face new charges along with them."

Sadness filled his heart. He prayed silently, "So, Lord, it's not an option now to finish the remaining five years in exile with my family, and I have to face a new trial and additional sentence? But I trust You even in this turn of events. Please help me to accept any outcome as from Your hand."

Three hours later the plane landed at the Moscow airport. Guards led him to a police car and drove to a local prison. There, as usual, he was searched and placed in a cell. That night he could not sleep at all and spent hours in prayer.

Friday, April 27, Moscow

The next morning a guard led Papa to a shower room, and all his clothes were taken to be deloused. Coming out of the shower, Papa found only his underwear and thought that the rest of his clothes were probably not ready yet.

The guard reappeared. "Vins, why aren't you dressed?"

"My clothes haven't been returned."

"But they're right here!" He pointed to a stool with a navy blue suit, white shirt, and neck tie on it. A new pair of shoes was also there.

"But those are not my things."

"Get dressed! They are here for you." ordered the guard.

Troubling questions formed in his mind. "What is going on? Who needs this masquerade in prison?" However, as a prisoner he had no choice but to obey the orders. As soon as Papa was dressed, the guard led him into an office. A man waiting there introduced himself as a government representative.

"Citizen Vins, by decision of the Supreme Soviet of the USSR, you are stripped of your Soviet citizenship! You will be deported to the United States today."

"But Russia is my homeland! On what basis are you stripping me of my citizenship?" Papa tried to object.

"For all your lawless activities!"

"I am a minister of the gospel. All my activities were entirely religious."

"At this point there is nothing left to discuss." the official interrupted. "Your outcome has been determined at a high governmental level. Remember, Vins, your foot will never again touch Soviet soil! Two hours from now you will be on your way to America."

124

Immediately following this exchange, the guards drove Papa to Moscow's Sheremetyevo International Airport. Inside the airplane, he noticed four other prisoners seated by the windows, each accompanied by two guards. Papa thought, "So I'm not the only one being deported!" The head of the convoy ordered him to take a seat by a window. Guards sat down beside him.

The flight lasted for almost ten hours. All kinds of thoughts kept running through Papa's mind. "What awaits me in that foreign land? How will I communicate, not knowing English? Will my family be allowed to join me?" His only comfort was in the Lord. As he had experienced many times during his prison life, Jesus remained unchanged even when everything else in life was falling apart. Now he trusted God to protect and guide him in the unknown land of America.

When they landed at the John F. Kennedy Airport in New York, all the passengers were invited to exit the plane. The prisoners and their guards, however, were told to remain seated. Then two Soviet spies, captured months earlier in the United States, were led into the plane. As they entered, the five former Soviet prisoners were allowed to exit.

On American soil, representatives of the U.S. State Department greeted them. They explained that a prisoner exchange arranged by the governments of the United States and the Soviet Union had just taken place. In the airport, reporters and TV cameras surrounded the group right away. After the initial interviews, the newly released prisoners were driven to a hotel in downtown New York where each got a room on the twenty-first floor.

When Papa closed his door, he was finally alone after a day-long journey that had begun that morning in a Moscow prison. He stepped to the window and looked down. It was almost midnight, but the brightly lit streets of New York City were churning with life. Everything was so unfamiliar and so foreign.

Saturday, April 28, Kiev

Meanwhile, back at home we were totally unaware of the events that had so abruptly changed Papa's life. Mama was still on her journey home from Tyumen. In a telegram that she had sent two days earlier,

Mama let us know that she had been permitted to see Papa in the Tyumen prison.

That Saturday morning Babushka, as usual, got up before everybody else. While she was fixing breakfast, the doorbell rang. "Who can it be so early?" she wondered as she went to open the door. There she saw Mama's younger sister Maria, who looked very excited.

"Have you heard the news?" Maria exclaimed without even saying hello. "Georgi is in America!"

Babushka tried to calm her down. "Maria, please come in. Sit down! Would you like some tea? Did you take a taxi to come here so early?"

"Yes, I took a taxi to bring you this news!" Maria replied.

As Babushka showed her to the kitchen table, she asked, "Now, what is this that you are trying to say? Who's in America? Nadia saw Georgi in Tyumen Prison just three days ago. She sent us a telegram."

"You just don't know yet. I was up at six and turned on 'Voice of America.' I heard on the news that five Soviet prisoners were taken from their prison cells and flown straight to America! Georgi was one of them! I roused Alexander so that he could hear it too. He told me to take a taxi and come and see you immediately."*

Babushka still could not believe it.

"It's not possible! We are packing suitcases to go into exile in Siberia."

"Turn on the radio and tune in to the next 'Voice of America' program. Then you will hear for yourself!"

Babushka woke everybody up. We did not fully believe the news until the next broadcast of "Voice of America." Then we even heard Papa's voice, as all five released prisoners were asked to say a few words of greeting to their families. After that we had no doubts that Papa truly was across the ocean.

---

*In those days there were not telephones in their homes.

Later that morning Mama arrived from Moscow. She took a taxi from the train station. As she rang the door bell, Peter opened the door.

"Do you know where Papa is?" he asked her right away.

"Oh yes, he is in Tyumen. I even got to see him! I found out that his exile will be in the village of Berezovo."

"Mama," Peter interrupted, "Papa is in America!"

"That's impossible! I saw him only three days ago in a transit prison."

Then Peter told her about the announcement on "Voice of America."

From that day on, events started to happen rapidly. On Monday several government representatives visited our house. They announced that, as part of an agreement between the two governments, our family had to join Papa in America as soon as possible. They handed us the applications that we had to fill out in order to leave the Soviet Union.

Babushka informed the officials that she refused to leave her homeland. "I'm already seventy-two years old, and it's too late for me to change my country of residence." They did not know how to react and left to consult with their superiors. Returning an hour later, the officials told Babushka, "Your whole family will go to America, no exceptions! If you refuse to go, we will carry you onto the plane!" She had to comply, and we all began filling out the forms.

The news that our family was leaving spread quickly among Christians. Friends from all over the country started to come to say goodbye. KGB agents parked a bus with curtained windows across the street from our house. From inside it, they constantly observed every person who came to see us. Many of our visitors were stopped and had to show their documents. Some were taken to the police station and searched. This tense situation lasted for six entire weeks until we left Kiev.

Our parting days remain fixed in my memory as quite unsettling. On the one hand, we were happy that Papa was finally free and that we would soon be reunited with him. But on the other hand, it was obvious that we were parting with our friends forever. Babushka felt this most acutely because the Christian prisoners, their families, and the ministry of the Council of Prisoners' Relatives, were an essential part of her life. Now all this would be left behind.

June 13, Sheremetyevo Airport, Moscow

On the day of departure, about forty friends came to see us off at the airport. They were from Kiev, Leningrad, Narva, Kishinev, Brest, and Voroshilovgrad. Our flight for New York left Moscow at 8:00 A.M. For some unknown reason, we were not allowed to board and had to wait for the next flight at 3:00 P.M. When the boarding was finally announced, our hearts were as heavy as if we were at a funeral.

Ahead of us lay something completely unknown and perhaps exciting, but it would be strikingly different from all that was familiar and dear back home. It was quite painful to cut off so drastically all the ties from the past, and yet we trusted in God's sovereign plans.

Epilogue

We landed at JFK Airport in New York on June 14, 1979. As soon as all the formalities with the immigration officials were completed, our hosts drove us into the night. An hour later, the lights of New York City were left behind, and we stopped to spend the night in a small country hotel. The next morning we continued our journey, and by late afternoon we arrived in Middlebury, Vermont, where Papa had been staying since his arrival six weeks earlier.

The first week in our new country, a small cottage in the mountains was rented for our family. That was what we most needed—to be away from strangers and spend time in our family circle. We enjoyed being with Papa again. He listened to our endless stories of the events back home, of parting with friends and of the farewell service in our church.

Papa also had a lot to tell us about his last days in prison, his shock at the announcement of his exile to America and of his first impressions here. But during those quiet days in a mountain cottage, we talked not just about the past. Papa shared his resolve to start actively helping the persecuted Christians in the Soviet Union. He was sure that that was why God in such a miraculous way had opened his prison door and brought him to freedom.

But although he was sure of God's specific assignment, in a practical sense he felt quite helpless. How could he start a ministry in a strange country where he did not even know the language? Among millions of Christians in America, who were his true friends? Where could he turn for help and advice? Only the Lord remained constant, while everything else in life had drastically changed. The challenge of being uprooted from all that was familiar and meaningful, from all that just simply made sense back home, in spite of the complexity of existence there, was at times quite unbearable.

As I look back today at the twenty-some years that have passed since our arrival in the United States, I realize how complicated was the adjustment to a new life. And yet time after time the Lord proved to be true to His promises, as He helped and provided for our family at each new turn. "For he hath said, I will never leave thee, nor forsake thee" (Hebrews 13:5). "For as the heavens are higher than the earth, so are my ways higher than your ways, and my thoughts than your thoughts" (Isaiah 55:9).

We got settled in Elkhart, Indiana, where God provided faithful new friends who helped Papa start the ministry that became the voice of the Persecuted Church.* The news that was reaching us in those days from Russia was troubling: pastors, Sunday school teachers, and other active Christian workers were being arrested, worship services were disrupted by the police, Bibles and Christian literature were confiscated during house searches, church buildings were destroyed.

Our mission started publishing the *Prisoner Bulletin*, a quarterly newsletter. We reported facts about persecution and gave guidelines that helped Christians in the West pray for the Persecuted Church, write letters of encouragement to prisoners and their families, and petition the Soviet government on their behalf. We published pictures of prisoners and their families and even included letters from prison camps.

As years went by and the ministry grew, the *Prisoner Bulletin* was regularly sent out to Christians in over fifty countries around the world. Papa was invited to preach in many churches across the United States, Canada, Argentina, Brazil, England, Switzerland, Germany, France, Holland, Sweden, Norway,† and Australia. The voice of the Persecuted Church was being heard throughout the world.

---

*Its initial name *International Representation* was later changed to *Russian Gospel Ministries*.

†When Georgi and Natasha Vins landed in Oslo airport in December of 1979, among those who came to welcome them was Dr. Alf Gerem, the Christian lawyer who had agreed to defend Georgi at his trial in Kiev in 1975, but was not granted by the Soviet government a visa to enter the country.

People used to ask what made the strongest impression when we first arrived in America. There were several moments that I will never forget. During one of the first weeks our family was invited to a Baptist church in Chicago. In the Sunday school hour, the pastor asked each of us a few questions through an interpreter. "What amazed you most in America?" he asked Jane. "Probably all the cars in Chicago? All the food in the grocery stores?"

She answered, "No, not the cars—we came from Kiev, the capital of Ukraine with a population of two million people and lots of cars, especially downtown. So, all the cars in Chicago isn't the most striking thing about America. The most amazing is freedom!" The pastor was quite surprised to get such a response from a fourteen-year-old.

For me, the strongest impression was made by a Christian bookstore. My sisters and I had tears in our eyes when we were taken to one for the first time. We gasped at all the Bibles—big and small, for children and for adults—displayed freely all over the store with no fear that the police could come and confiscate them. As we stood by the shelves full of Sunday school materials for children, I wanted to tenderly stroke the covers of all those wonderful books that Christians in my country were deprived of. Never before could I even imagine that such riches exist!

One Sunday we attended a Baptist church where over a thousand people gathered for worship. In the crowded parking lot little Alex suddenly exclaimed in Russian, "Look! Look at all these people! Everyone is carrying a Bible!" We all stopped and observed this powerful manifestation of freedom. Then during the service there was another moment that made a striking impression. At the beginning of his sermon, the pastor announced a passage of Scripture and asked the congregation to turn to it. As he waited, hundreds of people started to leaf through the pages of their Bibles. The quiet sound of turned pages filled the auditorium, and for me it seemed like the sweet music of freedom.

Soon the Lord provided the opportunity for my sisters and me to attend Bible colleges. As I sat in classes, absorbing the wonders of vast scriptural knowledge of Old and New Testament books, systematic theology, and church history, my heart filled with gratitude to the

Lord for making this possible. But I often wondered, "Why me, Lord? What about hundreds of my friends—young preachers, Sunday school teachers—why are they denied such a privilege?" So I started praying, "Please, Jesus, somehow—although I know how unrealistic this request is, my country being a stronghold of atheism, firmly closed to the Gospel—but I also know that nothing is impossible with You—please bring all these riches to my people!"

And the Lord answered! Eight years after I first prayed about it, God drastically changed the political situation in the Soviet Union, and I was able to go back to my country with professors from Bible colleges in America, and interpret for them at seminars where hundreds of Russian and Ukrainian Christians were enriched by solid biblical teaching. Only Almighty God was able to accomplish that!

My other dream since high school was to translate books. When at seventeen I gave my heart to the Lord, the opportunity for university training necessary for such a job was out of question. But when I came to America, God fulfilled that youthful dream too! After finishing Bible college, I started to translate Christian books from church history, missionaries' biographies, Bible commentaries, books on creation versus evolution, and children's books. This has been much more fulfilling than my girlish dreams of translating novels. Every book translated and printed by our mission was eagerly sought after, since very few Christian books existed in Russia after the mass destruction of such literature during the seventy years of communism.

As the years of our life in America went by, our family experienced times of grief and loss, as well as joy and celebrations. In 1985 we became U.S. citizens. That same year our grandmother Lydia died, and both Peter and Lisa graduated from colleges and got married. Jane was married in 1988, and our youngest, Alex, in 2000. Our parents' lives were enriched with seven grandchildren.

One of the greatest events in Papa's life happened in 1990, when Soviet President Mikhail Gorbachev retracted the decree that stripped Papa of his citizenship and exiled him to America. Finally, after eleven years of exile, Papa was able to return to his homeland. In November of 1990 he went back to Russia and Ukraine, and with joy unspeakable observed all the marvelous signs of freedom as he preached not just in churches, but in universities, prisons, schools, and open-air street meetings.

Papa discussed with church leaders from different cities how his mission in America could help the work of the gospel in this huge country where millions had never heard about salvation in Christ. Based on their requests, our mission started to collect funds for printing Bibles and other Christian books, for supporting pastors and their families, and for building churches mostly in small towns and villages. We also started to sponsor Christian summer camps, where many children accepted Christ as their Savior.

In the next seven years, Papa was able to go back to his homeland over twenty times, and preached in churches all over Russia, Ukraine, Belarus, Siberia and the Far East. He wrote and published several books based on his own and other Christians' prison experiences. Then, in the midst of an active ministry as he approached his seventieth birthday, he was diagnosed with an inoperable brain tumor.

On December 23, three weeks before he died, Papa asked me, "Natasha, please bring the manuscript of my new book. Let's finish working on it. I feel that this will be our last chance." We discussed each story and made the final decisions about the titles for each of them, and in which order they should be arranged in the book. After a couple of hours, he became quite tired and had to rest. I rearranged his pillows, gave him his medicine, and was about to turn the lights off and leave the room.

But he suddenly stopped me. "Could you sit down again? I would like to tell you more about my trip to the Ural Mountains in July."

With renewed energy he started telling me about this amazing opportunity to revisit the places where he had spent several years in prison camps thirty years earlier. He traveled to the Urals by car with two pastors from Kazan, Yury Trofimov and Gennady Elizarov. Their journey lasted for ten days and covered thousands of miles. Besides meeting with Christians, the highlight of the whole trip was visiting the headquarters of all the prisons in the Urals. Papa met with the chief officer and for a couple of hours shared with him the story of his own imprisonment and the reason for it. He was able to witness about God's love and redemption.

When Papa offered him the Bible and a book with his prison stories, the officer expressed his appreciation. When he learned that Papa had more books in his car, he asked if they could be presented to every officer on his staff. Pastors Elizarov and Trofimov, who had been waiting in the car, came in with the boxes of Christian books. Papa's next request to the chief officer was to leave with him all the extra New Testaments to distribute to the libraries of the prison camps in the area. The chief officer enthusiastically agreed to take care of it.

And now on his deathbed, only a few months later, with tears in his eyes Papa recalled this amazing incident. I was crying too. It was hard to believe that Papa's ministry had come to an end, and he and I had just worked on his last book. The trip he was telling me about was his last trip. Our conversation exhausted his strength, and I suggested that he rest. He agreed, but before I left the room he had something else to add.

"Natasha, my prayers are that the Lord will continue this ministry even after I'm gone. On our trip from the Urals back to Kazan with Yury and Gennady, several times we stopped the car as we approached a small town or just simply on deserted country roads in the forest. We would get out, kneel right there by the road, and pray for the Lord to send His laborers to all these towns and villages. And I know God heard our prayers!"

Papa fell asleep, and in the middle of the night his condition worsened. That evening was the last time he was able to carry on a conversation and to speak in full sentences. For the remaining three weeks he was drifting in and out of consciousness, speaking only short phrases. On the cold winter morning of January 11, 1998, his heart stopped beating, and the Lord welcomed Papa to glory.

I often think how inseparable each one of us is from our past and from the prayers that were offered up by loved ones who lived long before our times. My grandfather Peter Vins was shot in a Siberian prison in 1937 for preaching the gospel. He was thirty-nine years old. At home his wife and eight-year-old son longed to see him, not realizing that their reunion would be only in heaven. I wonder at times, what was on his heart and mind after he heard the verdict and was back in his cell awaiting the hour of execution? What did he pray about?

When Stephen was stoned, he saw "the heavens opened, and the Son of man standing on the right hand of God" (Acts 7:56). In this way Jesus Christ honored the dying moments of His faithful servant. I think, in the same way, He considered the last prayers of Peter Vins. Perhaps all that unfolded in Papa's life and ministry was the direct result of his father's prayers in that solitary prison cell in Siberia.

Over a decade has passed since Papa's homegoing. Russian Gospel Ministries merged with Frontline Missions International, a like-minded mission that has been helping to spread the Gospel in Poland, Albania, and former Yugoslavia.

In my life, once again, our Heavenly Father has proven that His great faithfulness endures to all generations (Ps. 119:90). While in Siberia in 2005, I met Alexander Velichkin, a Russian evangelist who for two decades has taken the Gospel to the remotest villages along the Siberian rivers, reaching groups of people that have never heard of Jesus. No roads are there; people live along the rivers, which are the only way of communication. Villages are small and are hundreds of miles apart, surrounded by *taiga*, the huge Siberian forest.

Now Alexander and I are married. We serve as missionaries with Evangelical Baptist Missions in northern Siberia. God opened this door of opportunity (1 Cor. 16:9) that continues my father's vision to take the gospel to the remotest parts of Russia.

> "O the depth of the riches both of the wisdom and knowledge of God! how unsearchable are his judgments, and his ways past finding out! For who hath known the mind of the Lord? or who hath been his counsellor? Or who hath first given to him, and it shall be recompensed unto him again? For of him, and through him, and to him, are all things: to whom be glory forever. Amen."
>
> Romans 11:33–36

> "О, бездна богатства и премудрости и ведения Божия! Как непостижимы судьбы Его и неисследимы пути Его! Ибо кто познал ум Господень? Или кто был советником Ему? Или кто дал Ему наперед, чтобы Он должен был воздать? Ибо все из Него, Им и к Нему. Ему слава во веки. Аминь."
>
> Римлянам 11:33–36